MEN

... FOR WOMEN ONLY

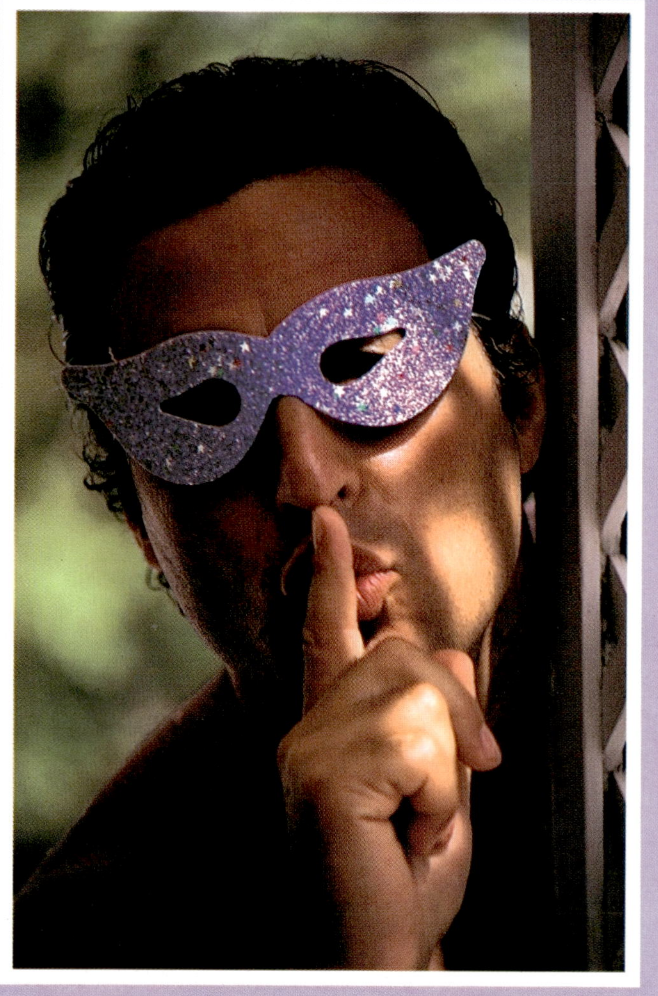

MEN

...FOR WOMEN ONLY

GRY IVERSLIEN

WORDS BY JUSTIN DE VILLENEUVE

COLUMBUS BOOKS
LONDON

For my girlfriends:

Sharon Oppenheimer
Jan de Villeneuve
Elly Arnstein
Denise Magalhães
Marianne Holtermann

Note The verses in this book are free poetical fantasies which have no direct connection with the subjects of the photographs

First published in Great Britain in 1988 by
Columbus Books Limited
19–23 Ludgate Hill, London EC4M 7PD

British Library Cataloguing in Publication Data
Iverslien, Gry
Men ... for Women Only
1. Photography. Social subjects:
Men – collections from individual artists
I. Title II. De Villeneuve, Justin, *1939–*
779.23

ISBN 0 86287 324 X

Designed by Simon Balley Design Associates

Printed and bound by arrangement with
Graphicom SRL, Vicenza, Italy

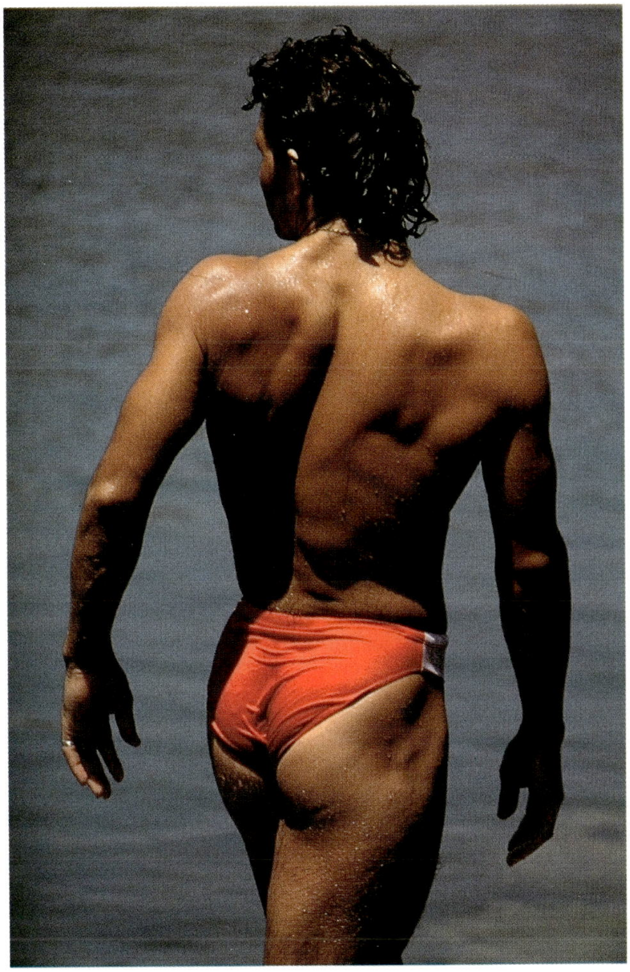

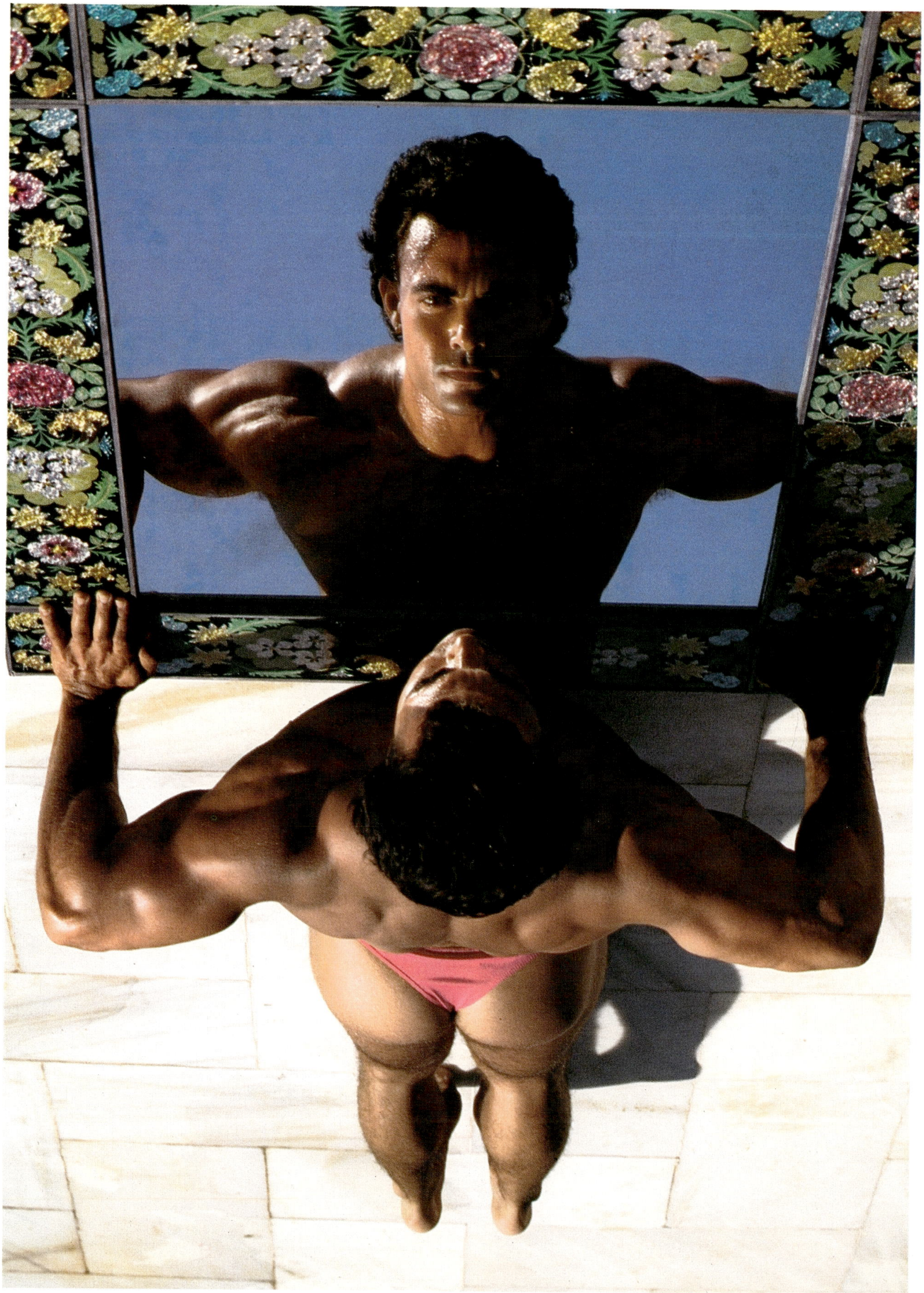

FOREWORD

The idea for this book emerged entirely by chance...

As a photojournalist I am snapping pictures almost constantly; one day I shot one of a friend of mine relaxing by a swimming pool. This image, of a handsome man wrapped in a yellow towel, sipping orange juice and bathed in sunlight, soon became, of all the pictures in my portfolio, the one strongly favoured by my girlfriends—so much so that they would sometimes drop in on any excuse, just to take another look at this particular photograph.

Their interest initially amused me, but it also indicated that there was clearly a demand for this kind of image. The popularity of that picture became the initial impulse for an obvious and seemingly simple idea: *Men ...for Women Only*.

I searched bookshops and libraries for similar or related publications, but although I came across scores of photographic books on women, any number of glamorous females in a vast range of guises and settings, there were hardly any photos of men. By now I was building up enough confidence to tackle the project myself—a whole book devoted to men.

From the very beginning, I had a very strong conception of what the book should stand for and what it should not. I was not going to seek revenge for all the years men had exploited my own sex. On the contrary, I wanted to show appreciation, even admiration; I wanted to present a portfolio of high-quality photographs, strong images of a wide range of men, with subtle hints of sensuality and attraction and with a sense of atmosphere.

I did not want to show just the beach-boy type; I did not want my subjects to look either ridiculous or vulgar, nor did I want to see them lounging nude over the bonnet of a fancy car. I also wanted to avoid the somewhat sterile fashion-shot image.

Instead, I was after something rather like a good-quality snapshot: a movement, a glance, a situation, captured at a particular moment, seen through the eyes of a woman and showing a man who is fully aware of being in the presence of a woman.

With this in mind I ventured forth, starting with my immediate circle of friends, but branching out eventually to include men of many nationalities and from various walks of life, and I shot pictures over a period covering four seasons.

I only hope that you have as much fun looking at these pictures as I had taking them.

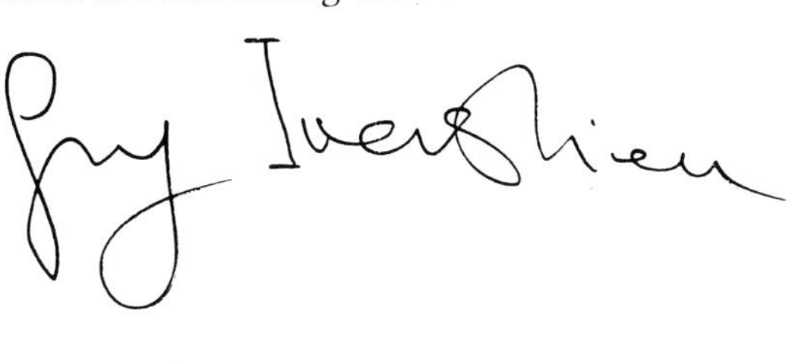

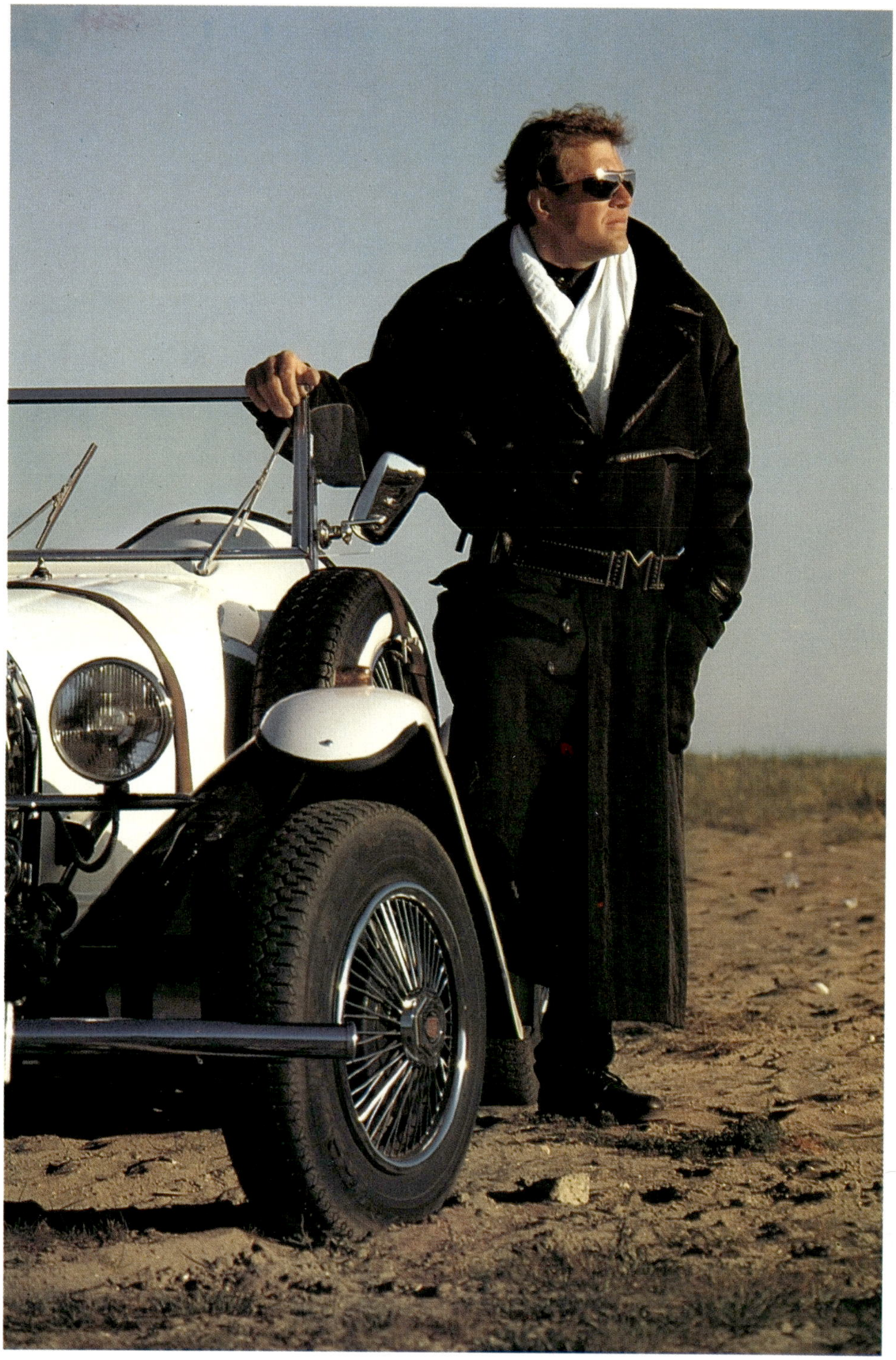

He stood there by his sports Bugatti
Like a White Russian from Togliatti
He even wore a Russian coat
A cashmere scarf graced his throat
He offered to drive me to Bukovina
Or fly me to Argentina
Sail to Barcelona, or overland to Arizona
What could I say? … Ochi chornia!

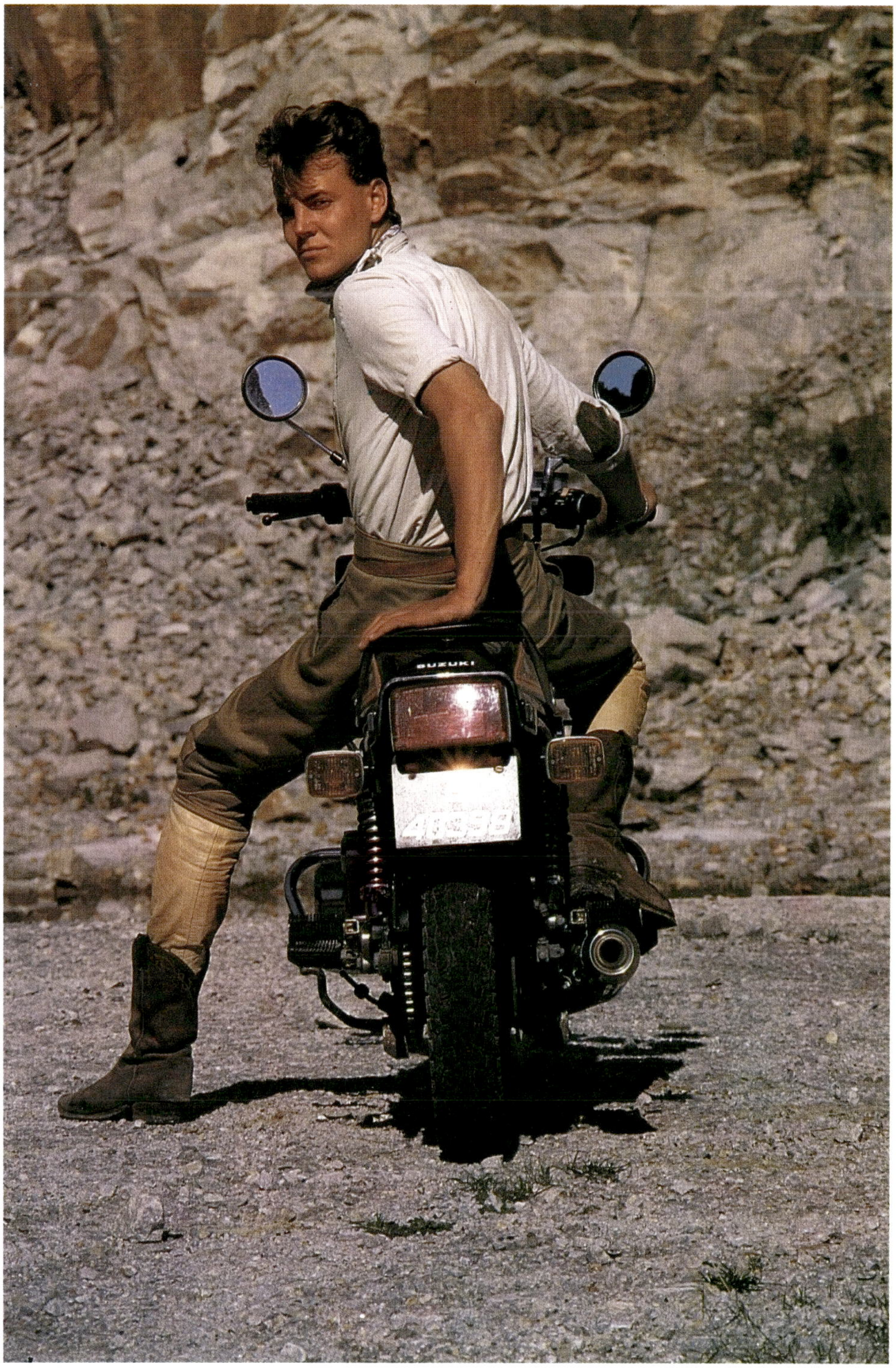

The Teutonic tearaway sat astride his bike
Would I sit on the pillion?
Well, why not, if he likes

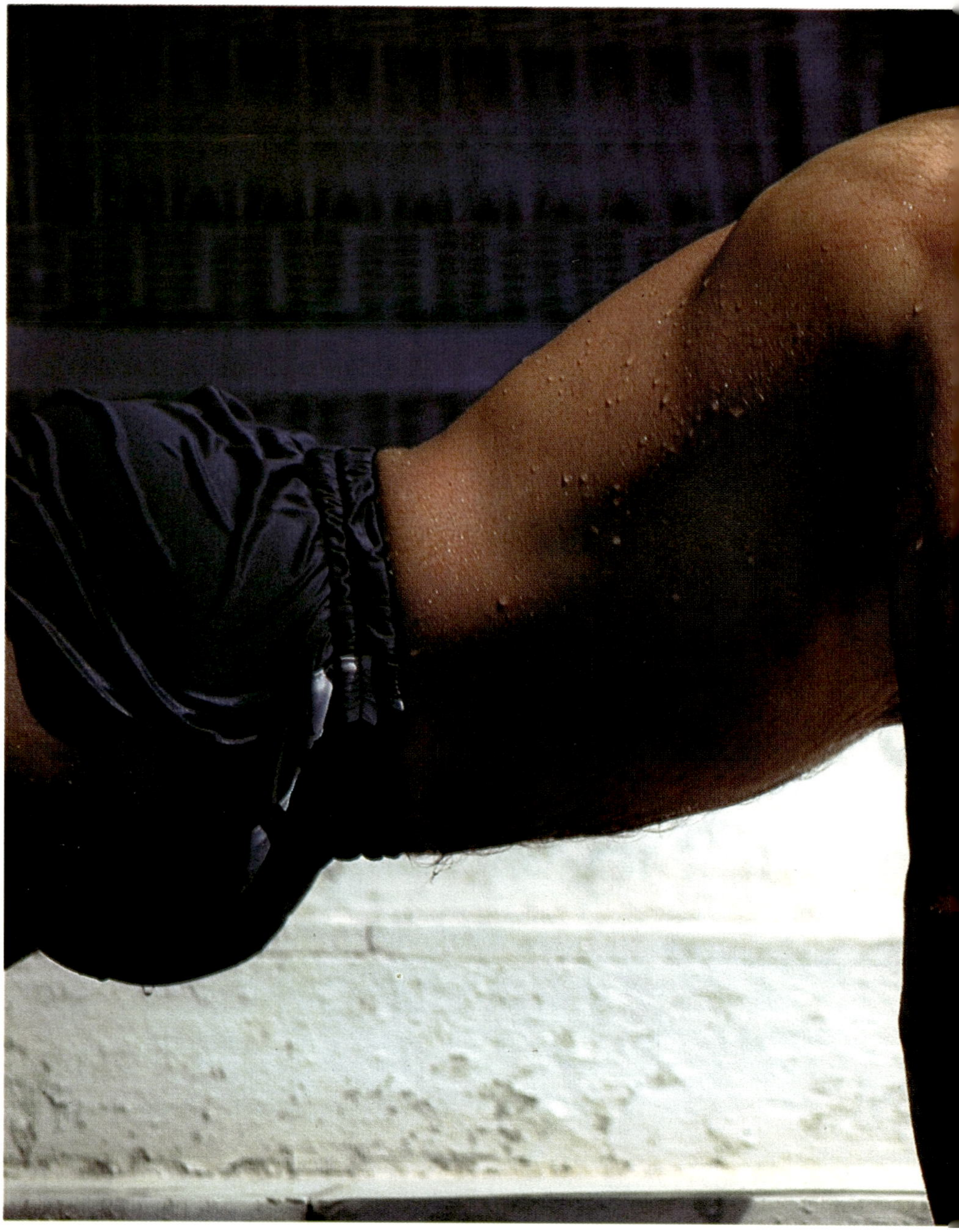

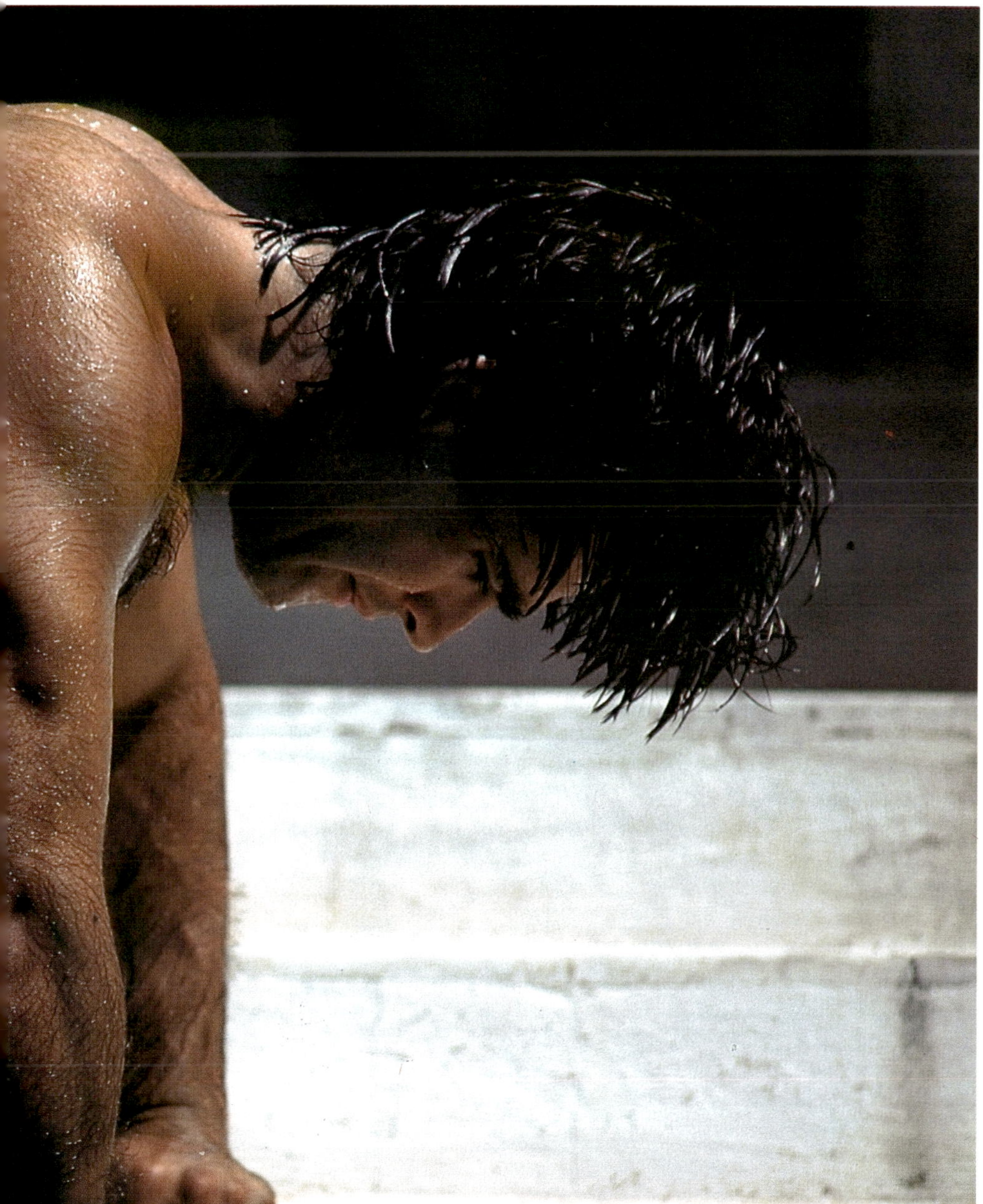

This muscleman was very fit
He should really take it easy
He uses up such energy
... Hope he keeps some back for me

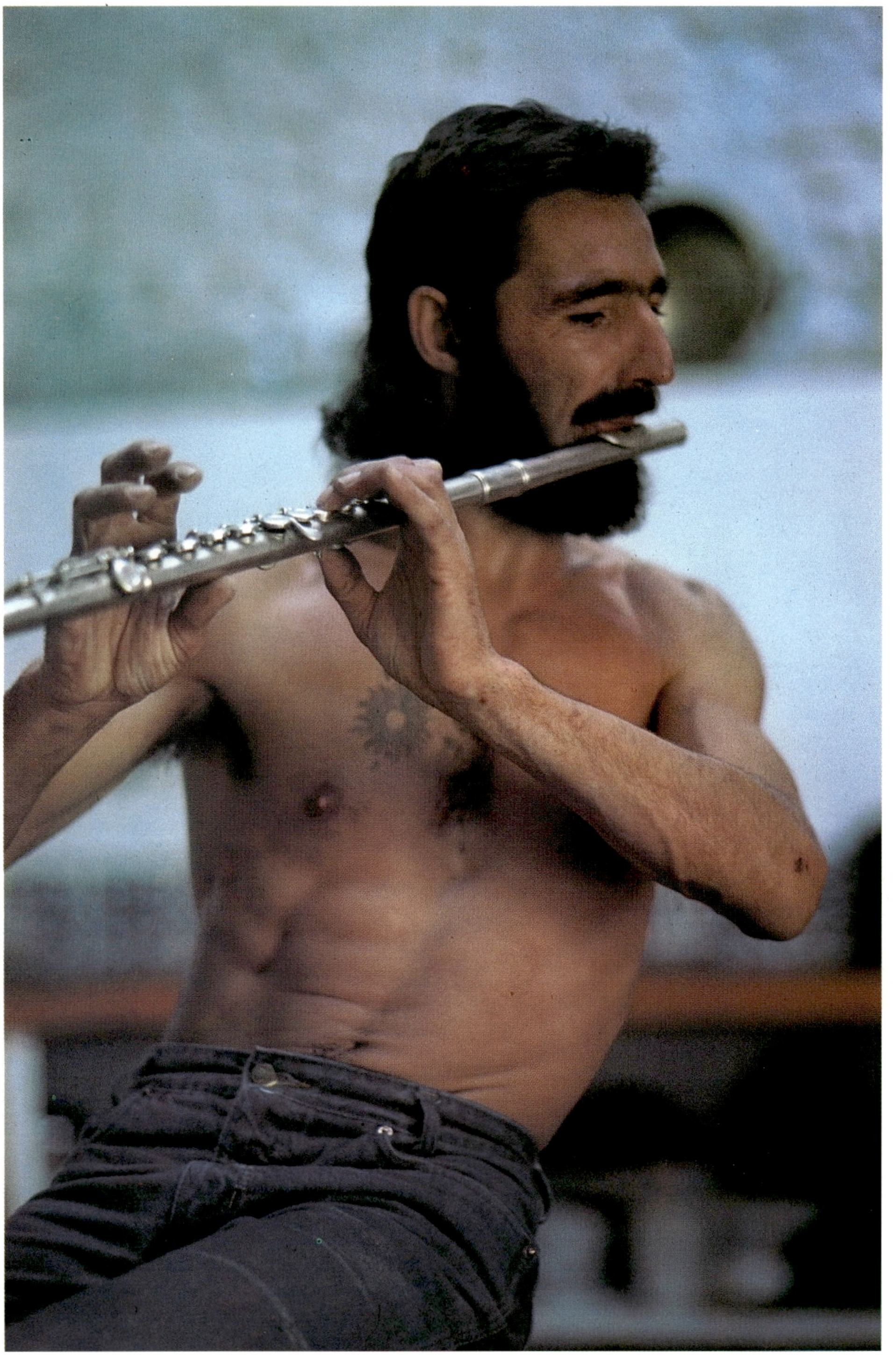

I'd really like to spend some time
With this mystery man of mine
Perhaps we'll go to Katmandu
Ending up in Old Peru
Turkestan, or Abadan for Ramadan
There's lots of things that we could do
... Let's start with that wild tattoo

He ran his bow across the strings
Of the lapis-blue violin
His touch was soft and gentle
My heart began to sing
Would he play a tune for me?
I'd listen to anything

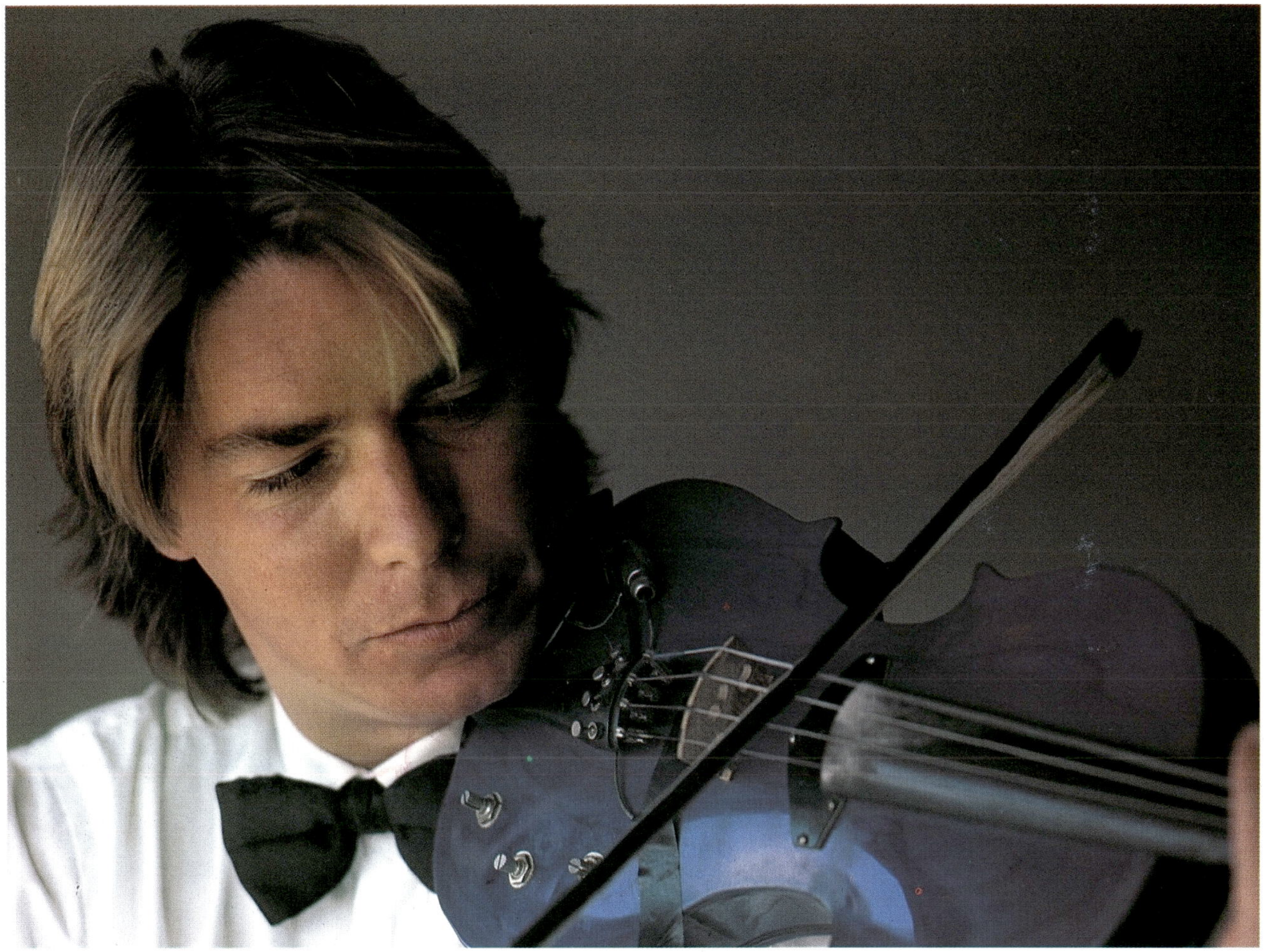

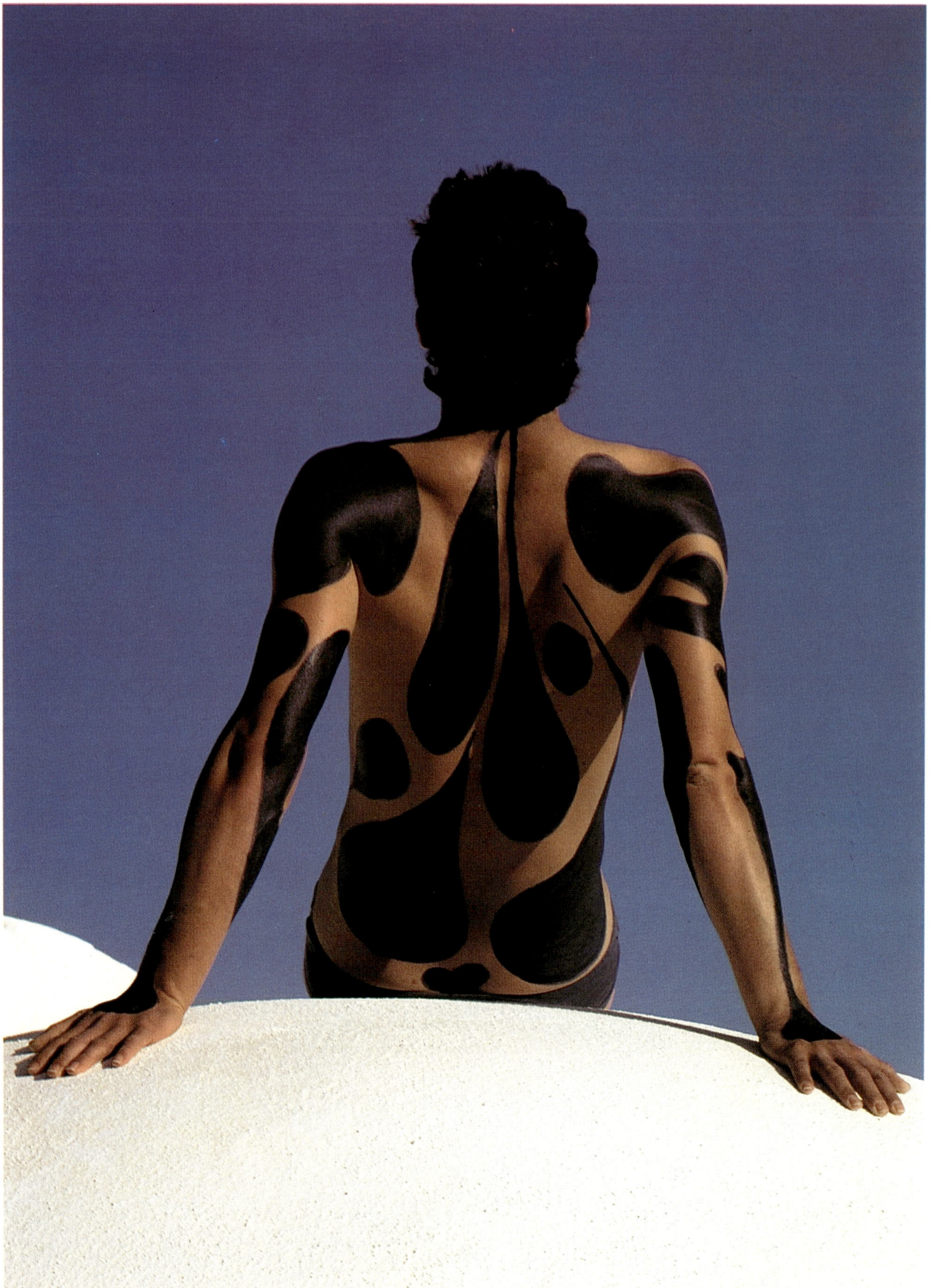

The young man was quite a sight
He really looked bizarre
I know some women like tattoos
But he's gone somewhat too far

He looks a serious boy
Assessing a piece of sculpture
But I'm sure he likes a bit of fun
When the day is over

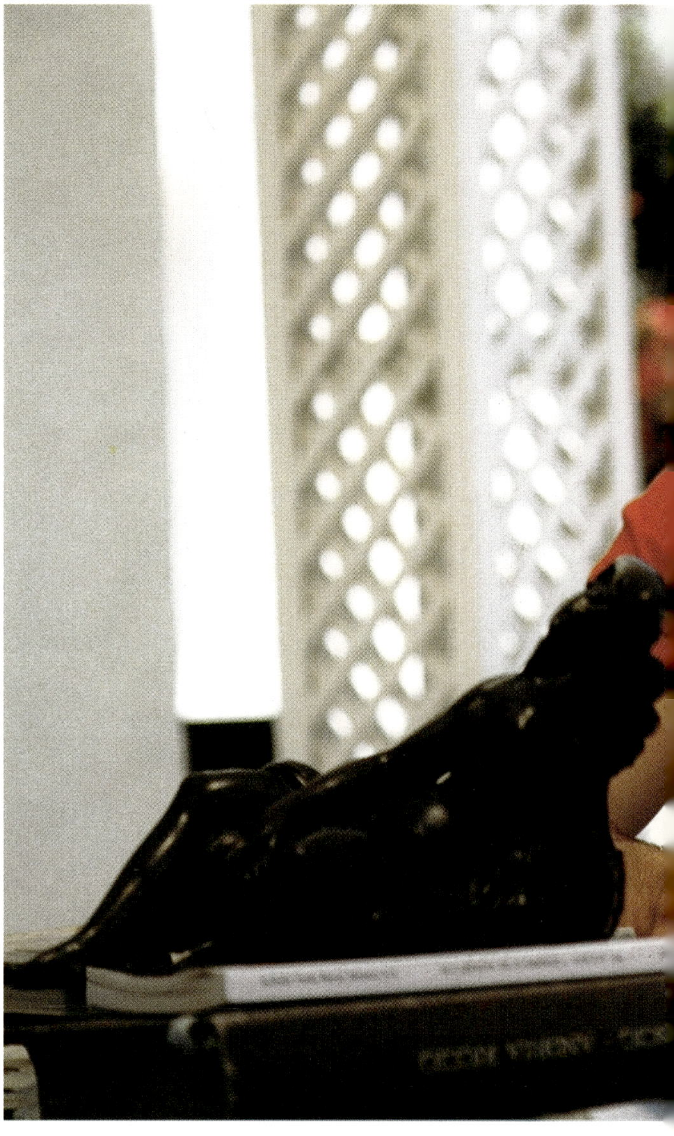

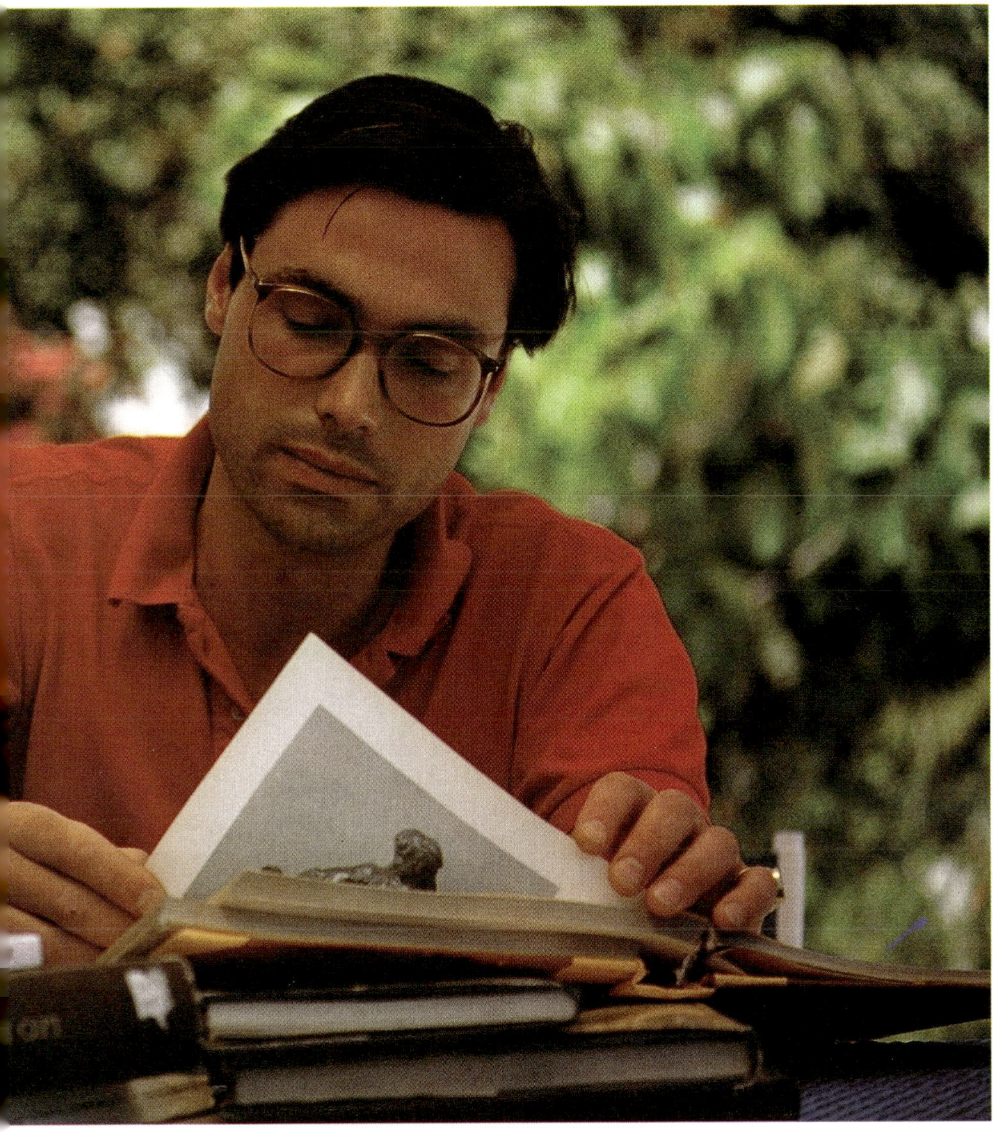

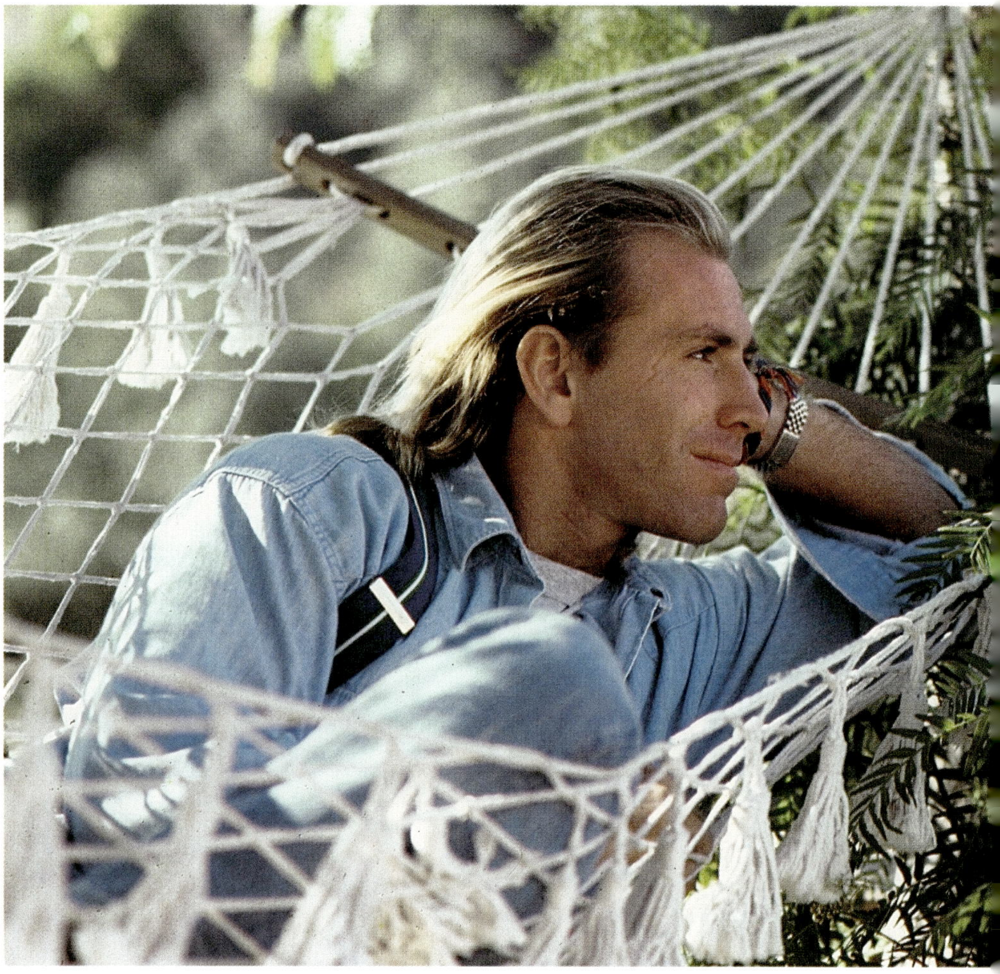

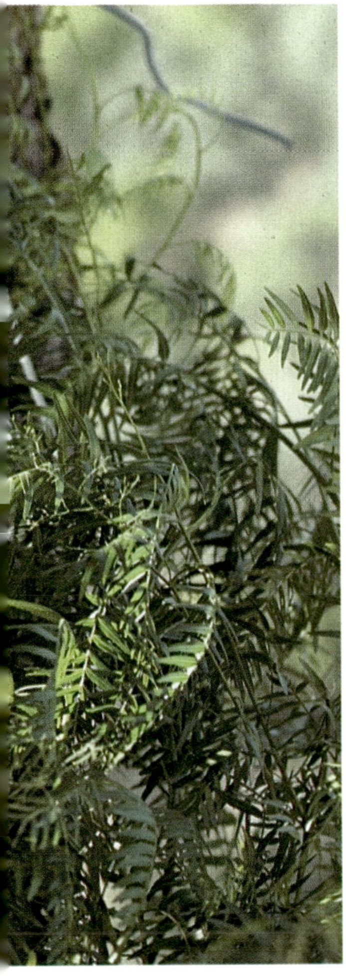

This young man was swinging in the breeze
His bed strung up between two trees
I wonder if another could get in
With a squeeze ... Please

I saw him taking photographs
One of those fashion shoots
He looked a lively fellow
... with or without his boots

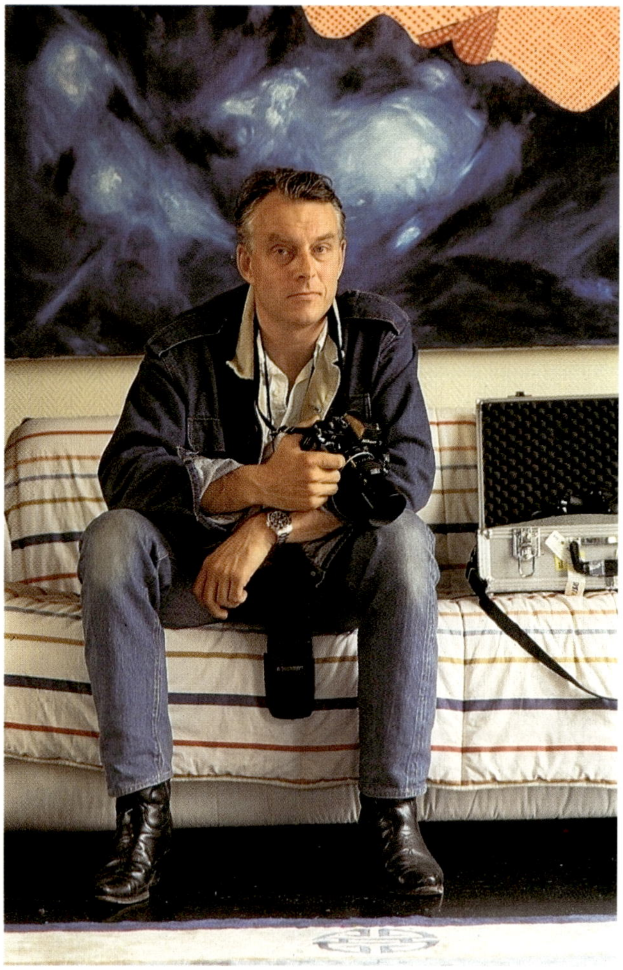

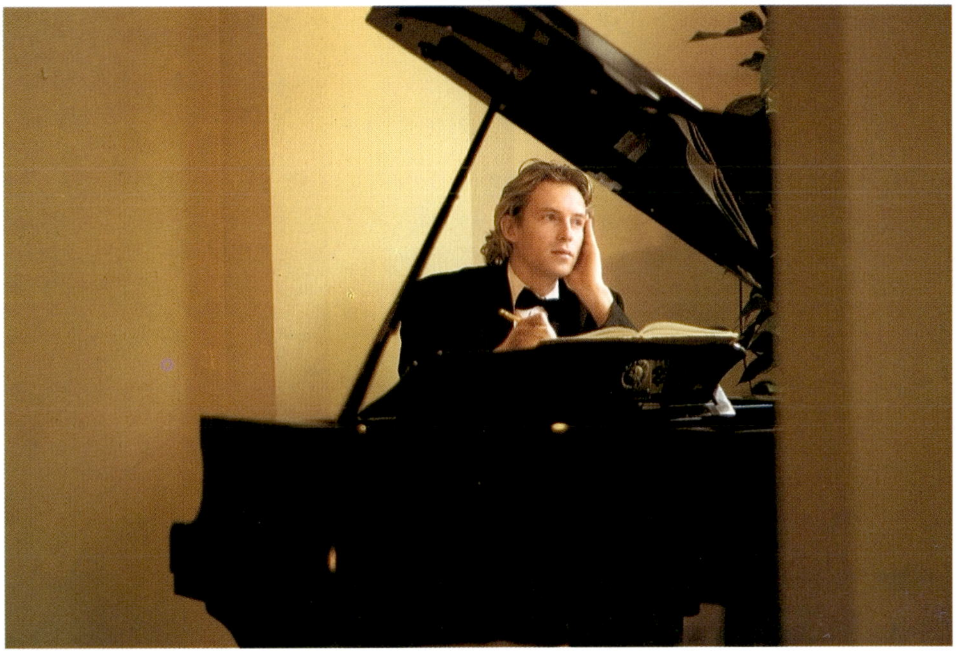

With elegance and agile ease
The young man's hands brushed ivory keys,
What rhapsodies and melodies
The waltzes of the Viennese ...
Oh, to join him in romantic reveries

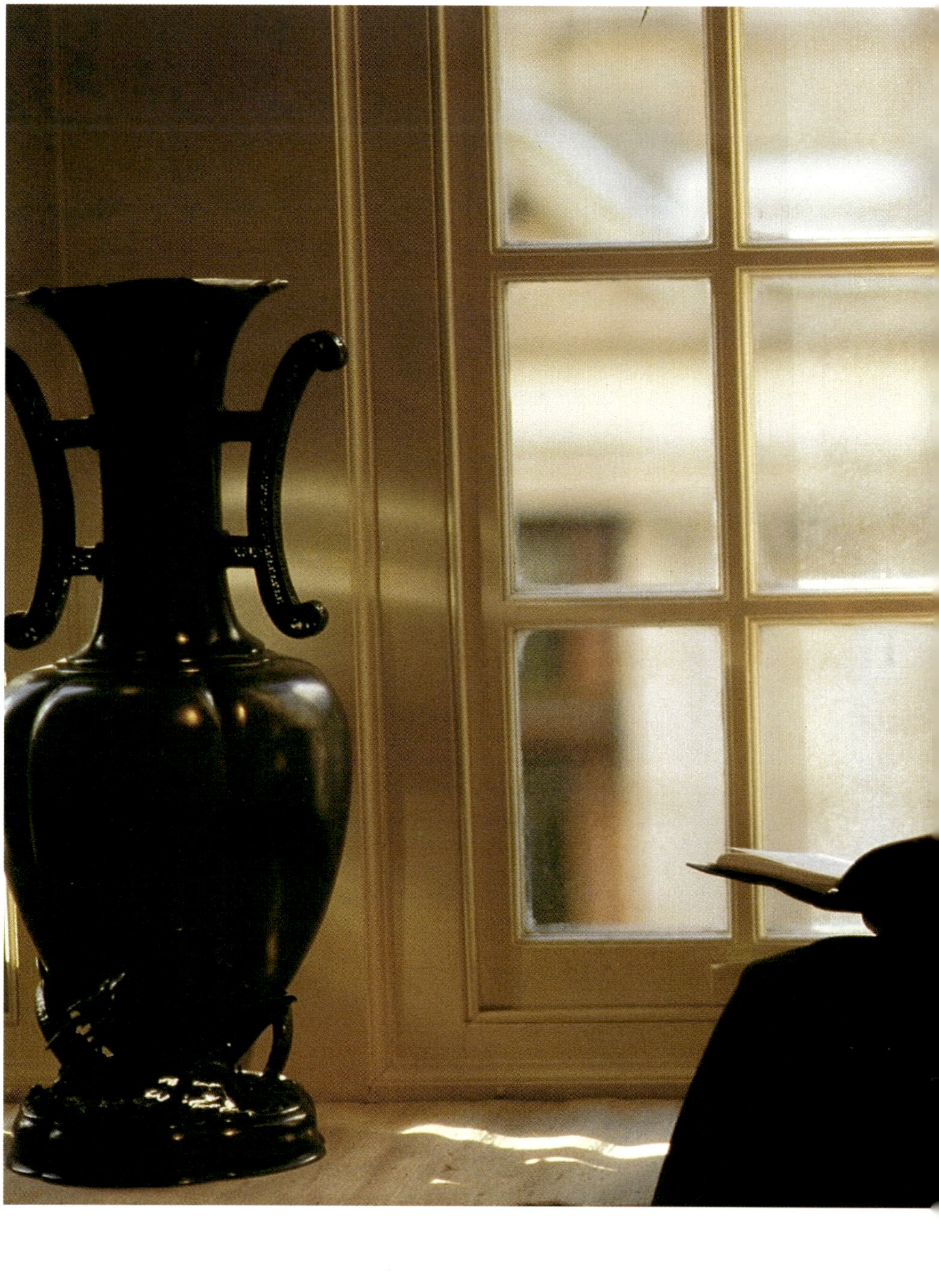

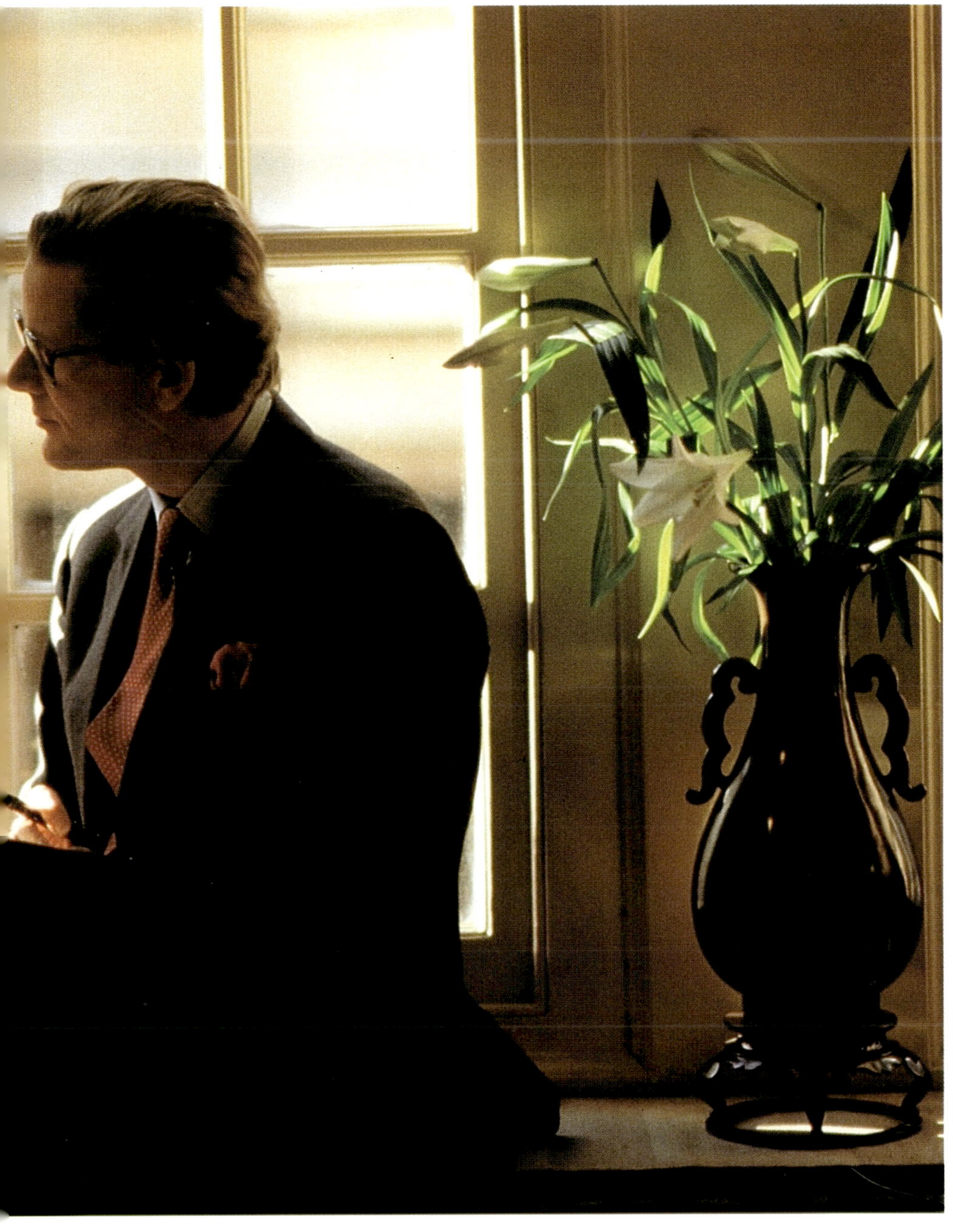

It never ceases to amaze
The thoughtful gaze on ancient vase
Perhaps I could change his ways
... Maybe I'll unhook my stays

Is this a literary man
Does he study words and prose
Descartes or primitive art
... or does he only like to pose?

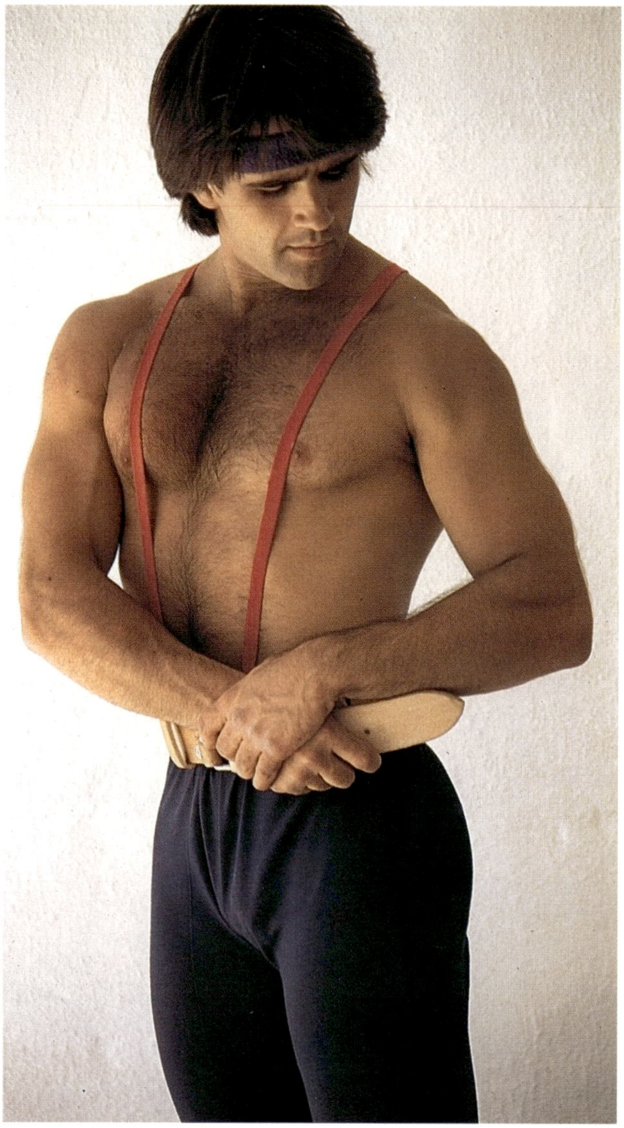

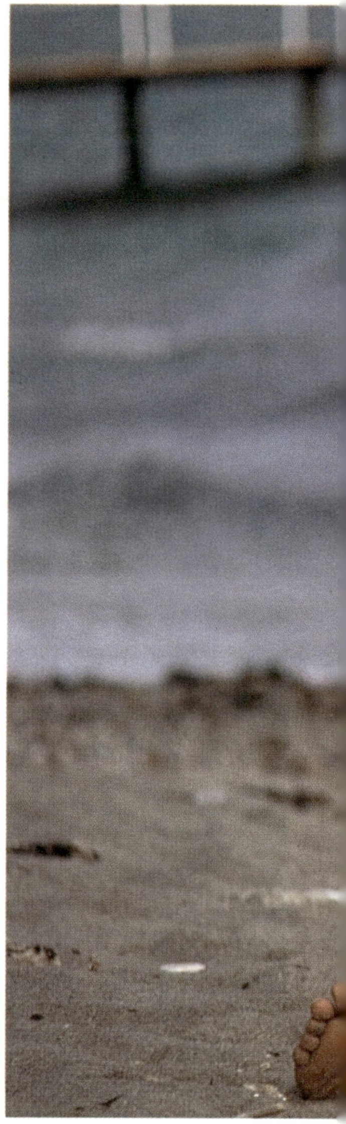

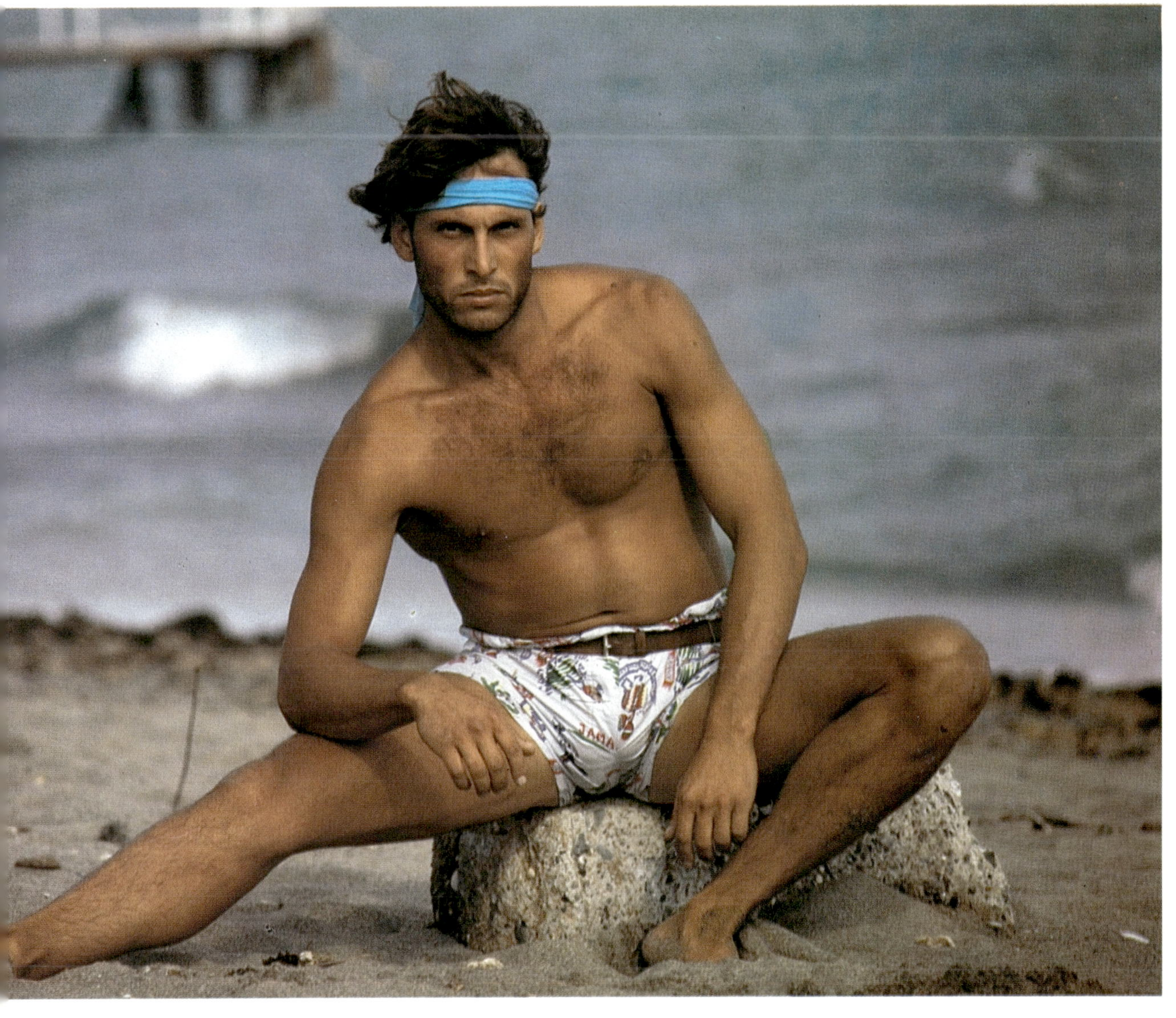

This gentleman's American
Although he's far from home
I don't know who he thinks he is
But I'd guess it's Sly Stallone

This could be the man for me
A little like Sean Connery
Perhaps he'll turn into James Bond
... If he waves his magic wand

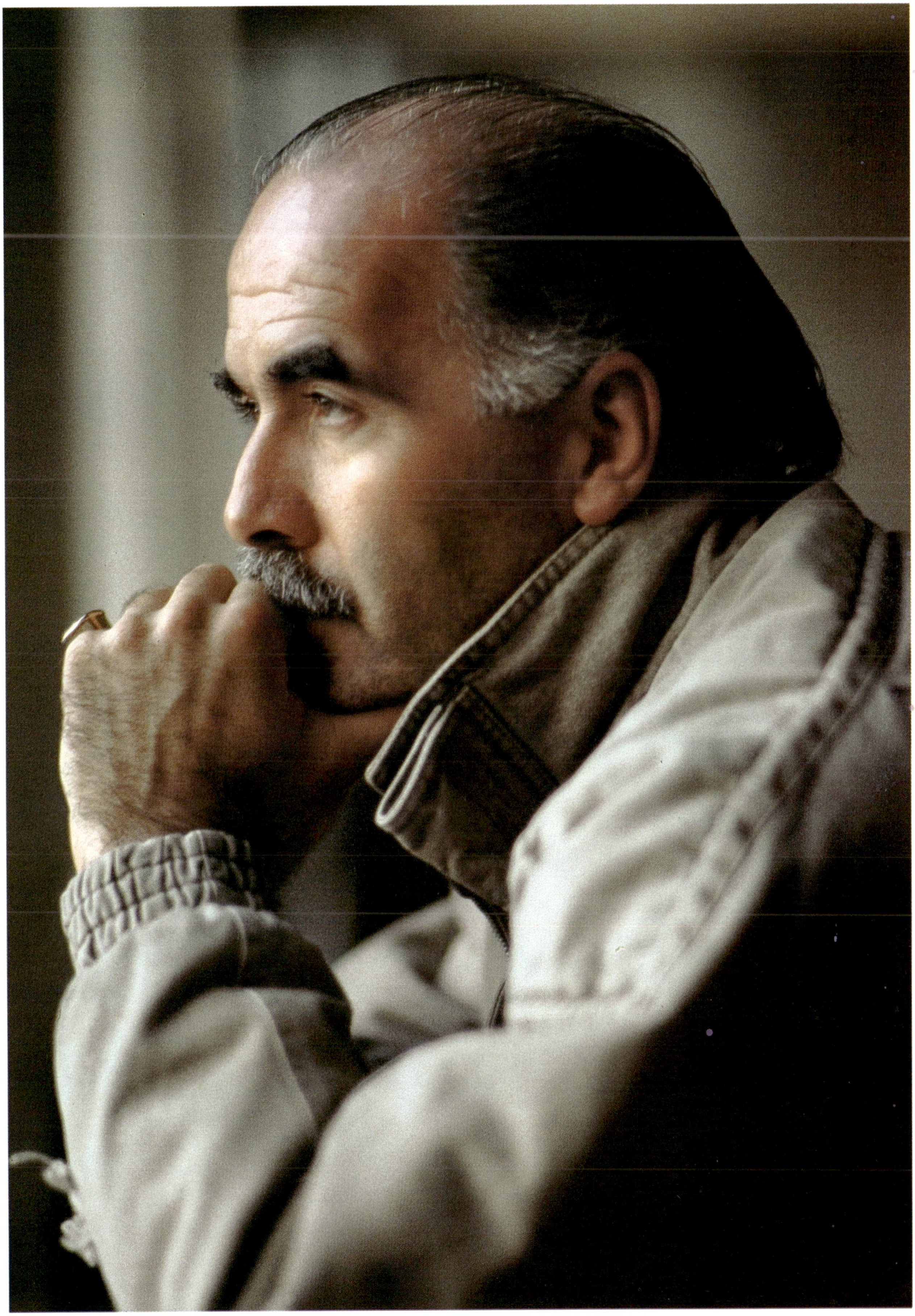

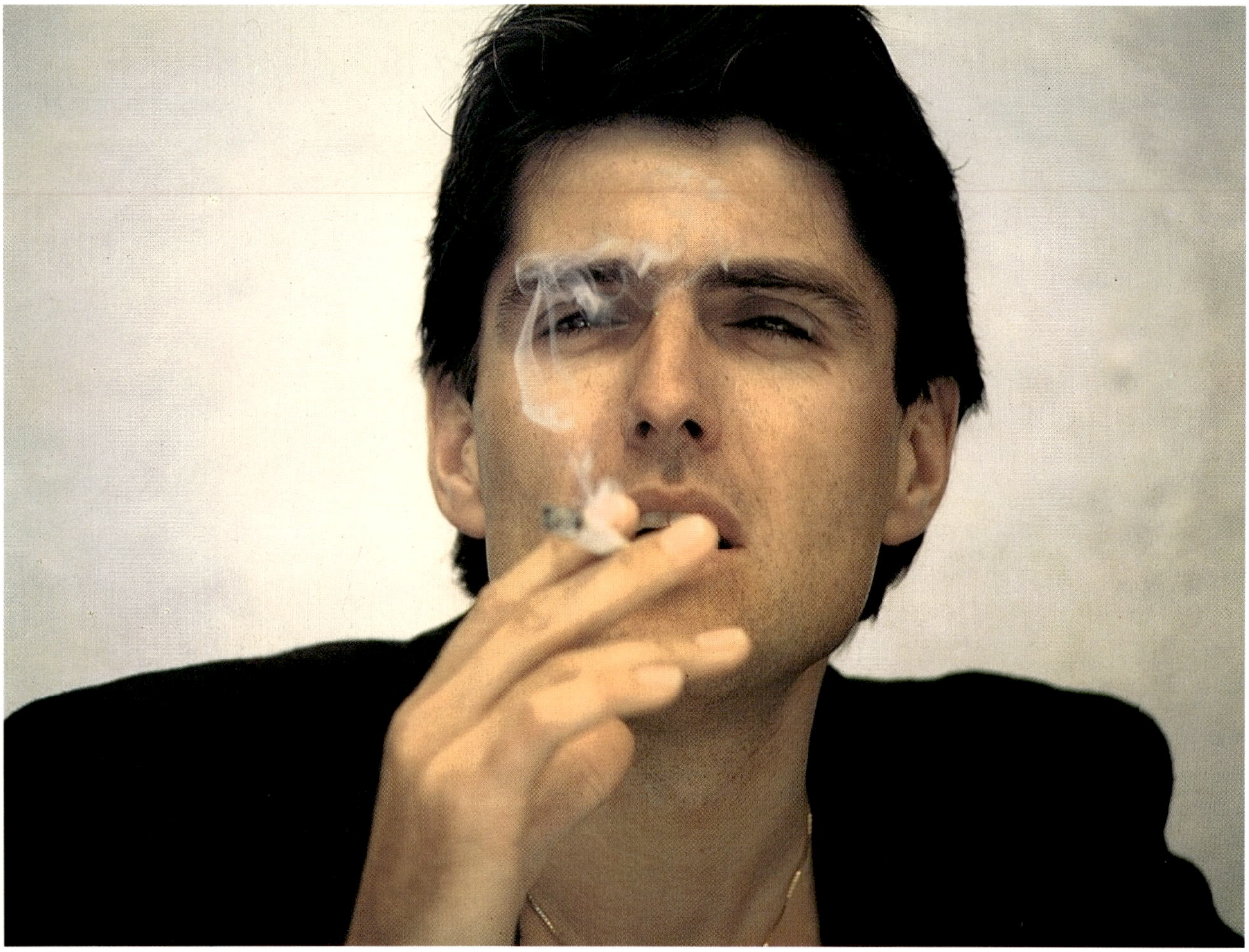

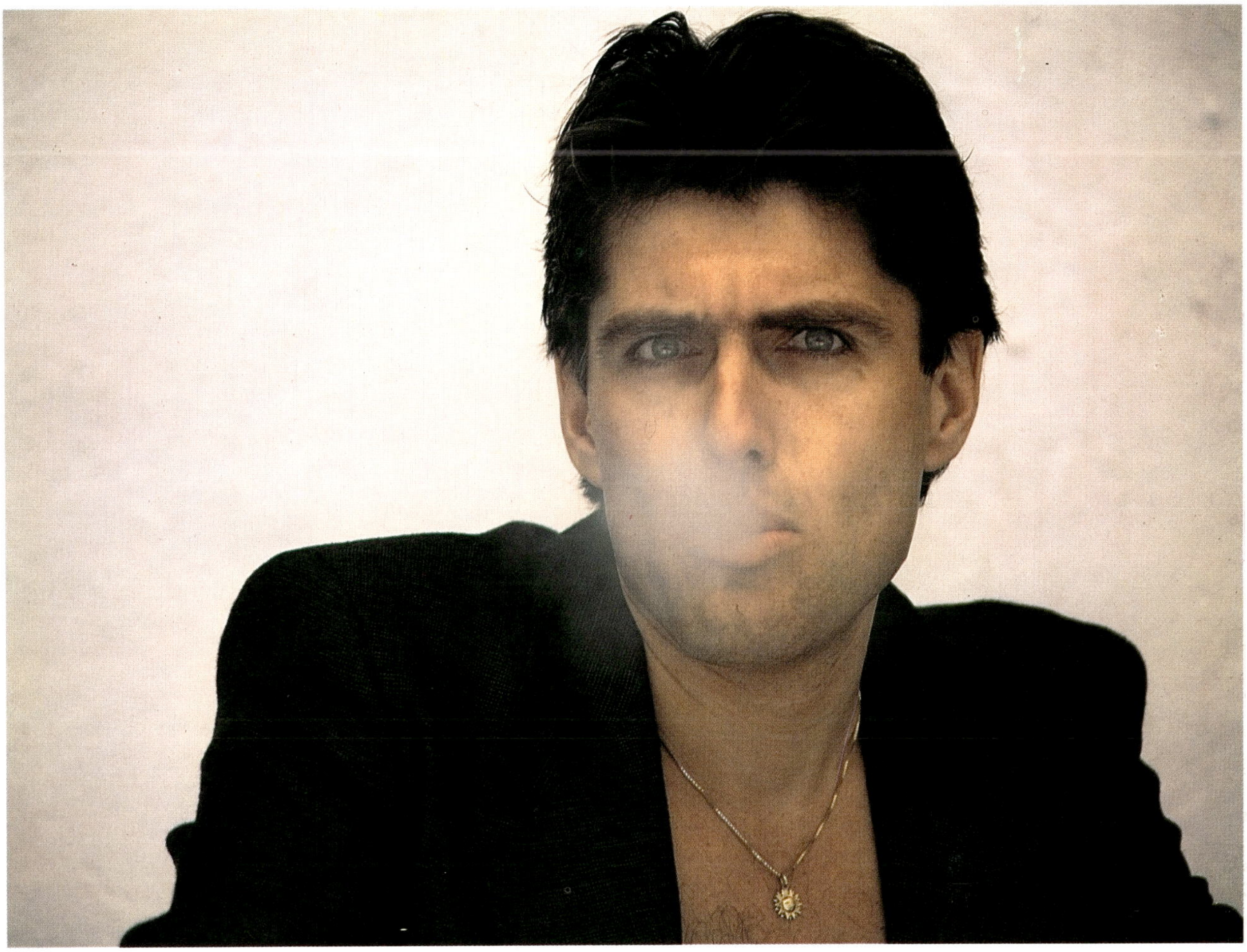

This dark-eyed young man liked a smoke
And I knew before we even spoke
That he could get much bolder
And when he put his ciggy out
He'd do much more than smoulder

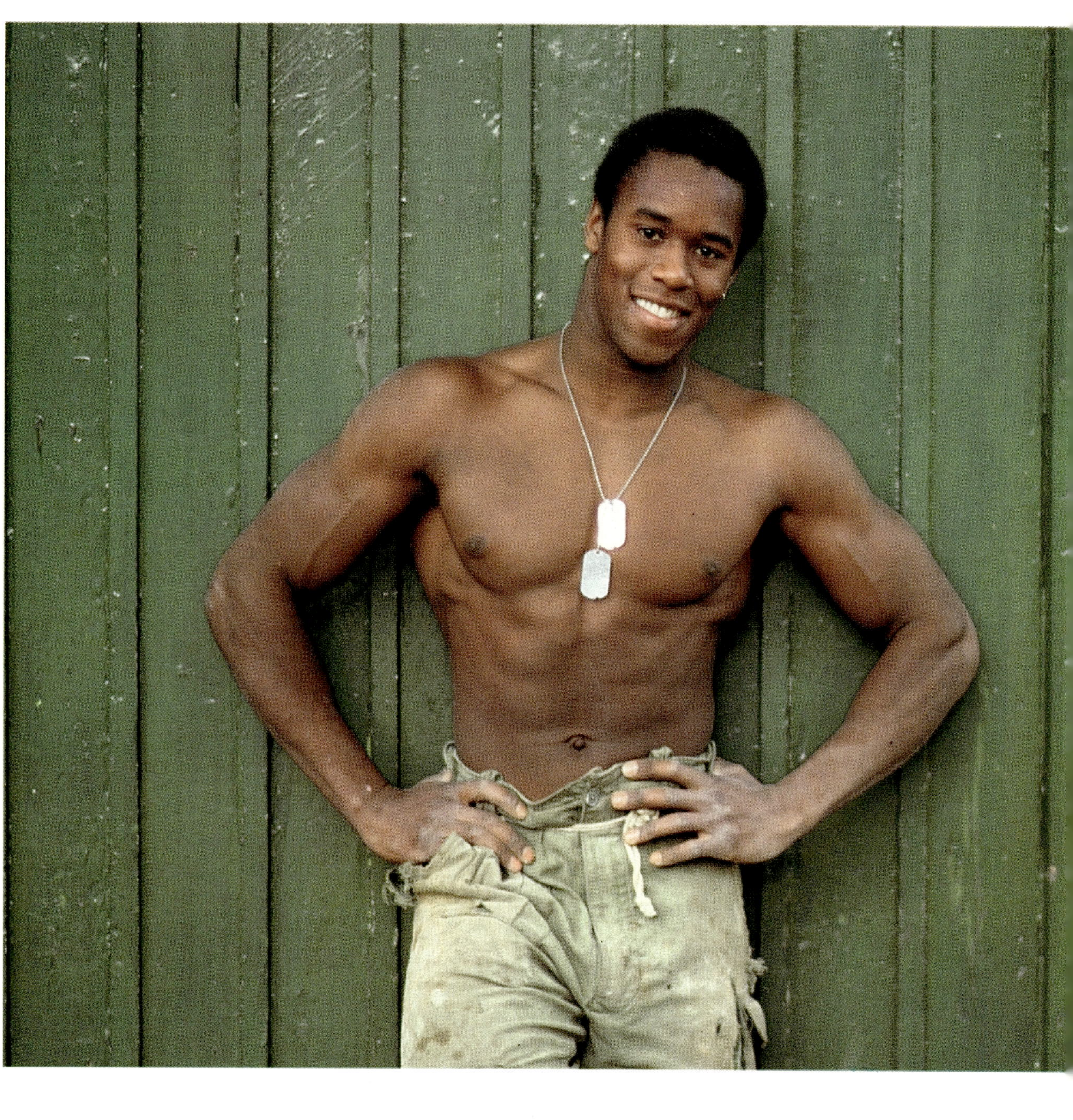

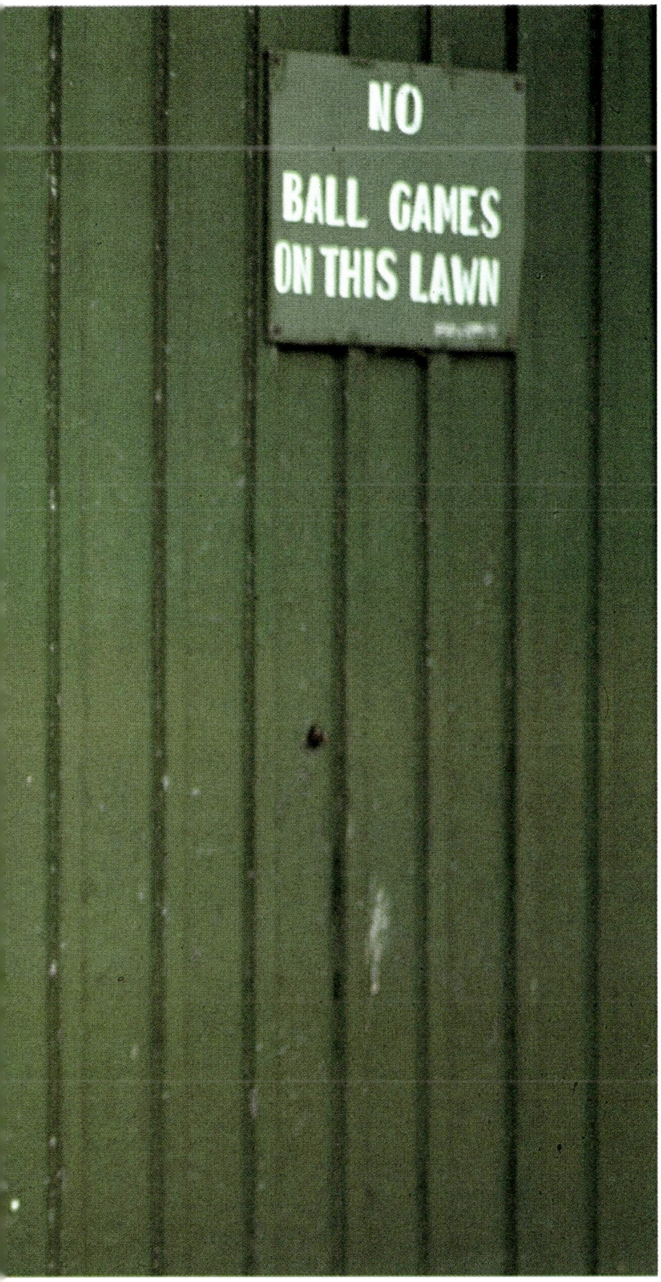

I loved the way the sun shone down
on his beautiful golden skin
His carefree nonchalant attitude
The wonderful mischievous grin
There was something about
the way he moved
What more can I say?
Olé *for* café au lait

This young man had a naughty look
I had a touch of déjà-vu
Was it a film, or was it a book?
Suddenly I knew
Albert Finney in Tom Jones
Where he wore a powdered wig
And just like old Bertie boy
This one was fresh as his fig

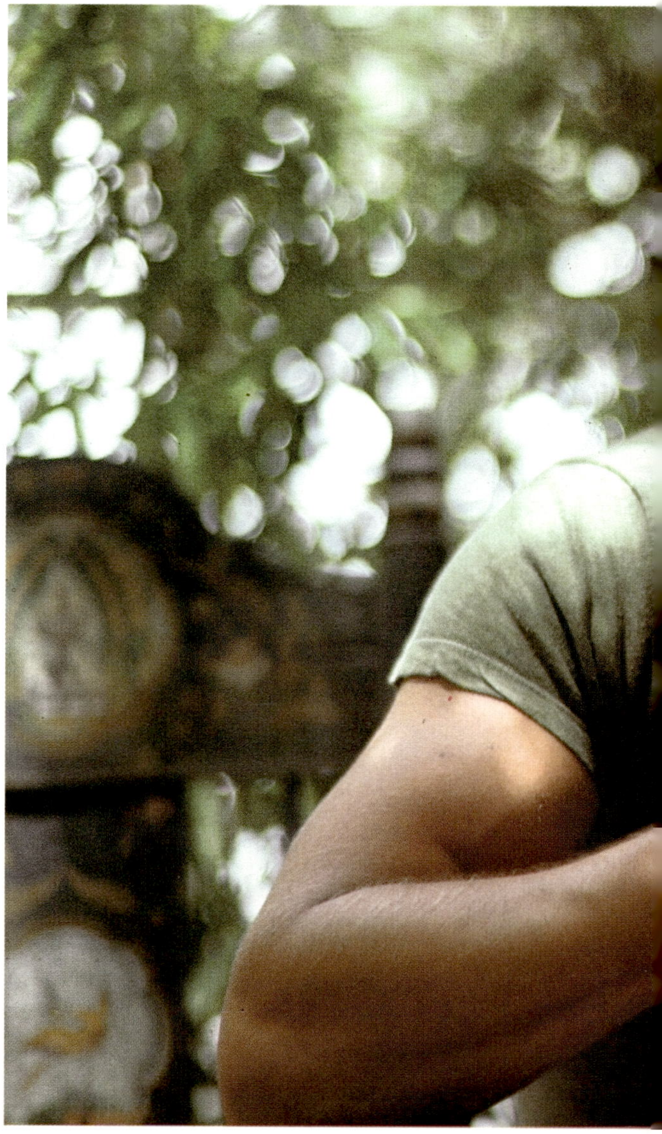

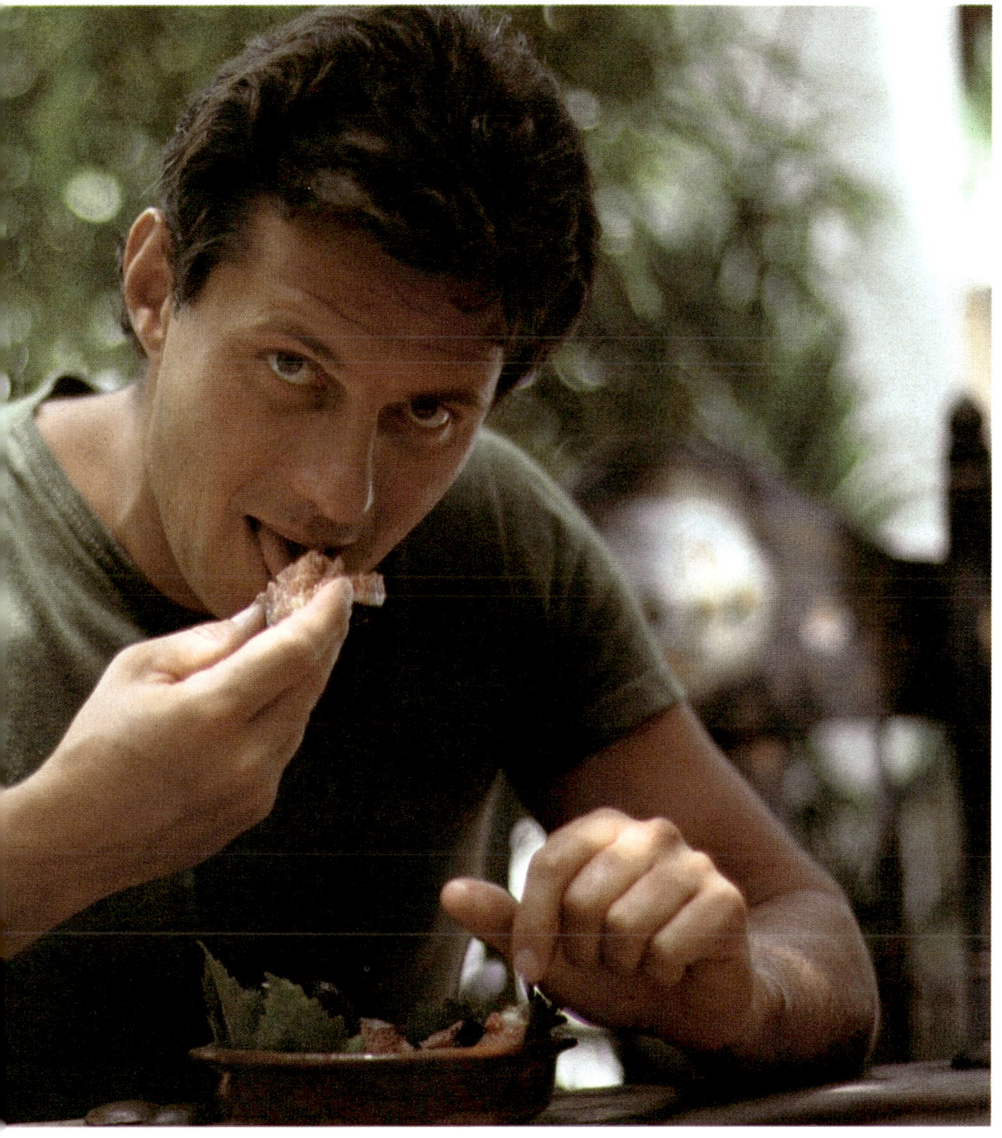

When I first spied this gentleman
With classic style and grace
I wondered, was he Roman or Greek?
One can't tell by his face

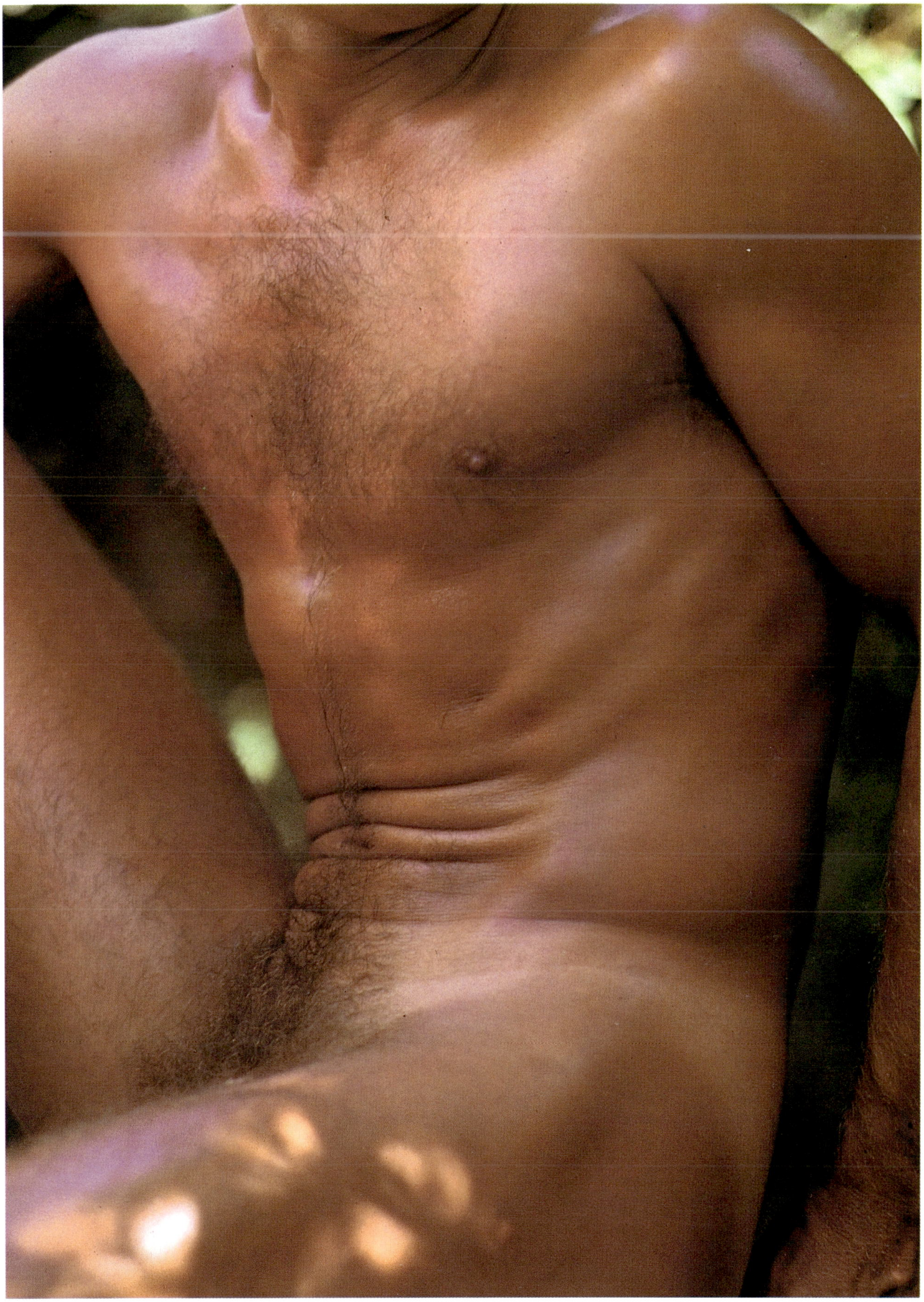

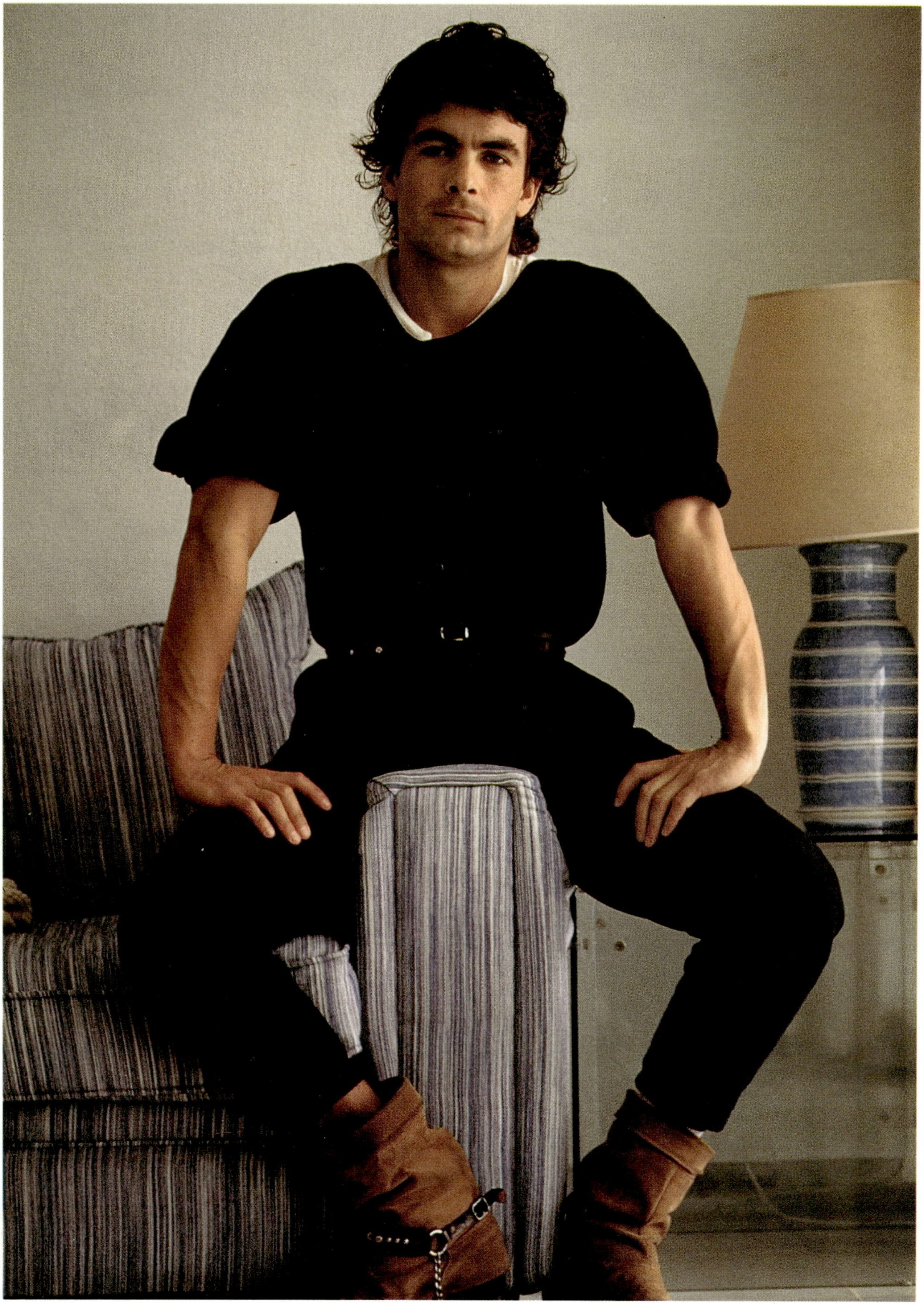

Tall, dark and handsome
This chap looks very fit
Perching on the sofa
... I have to have his portrait

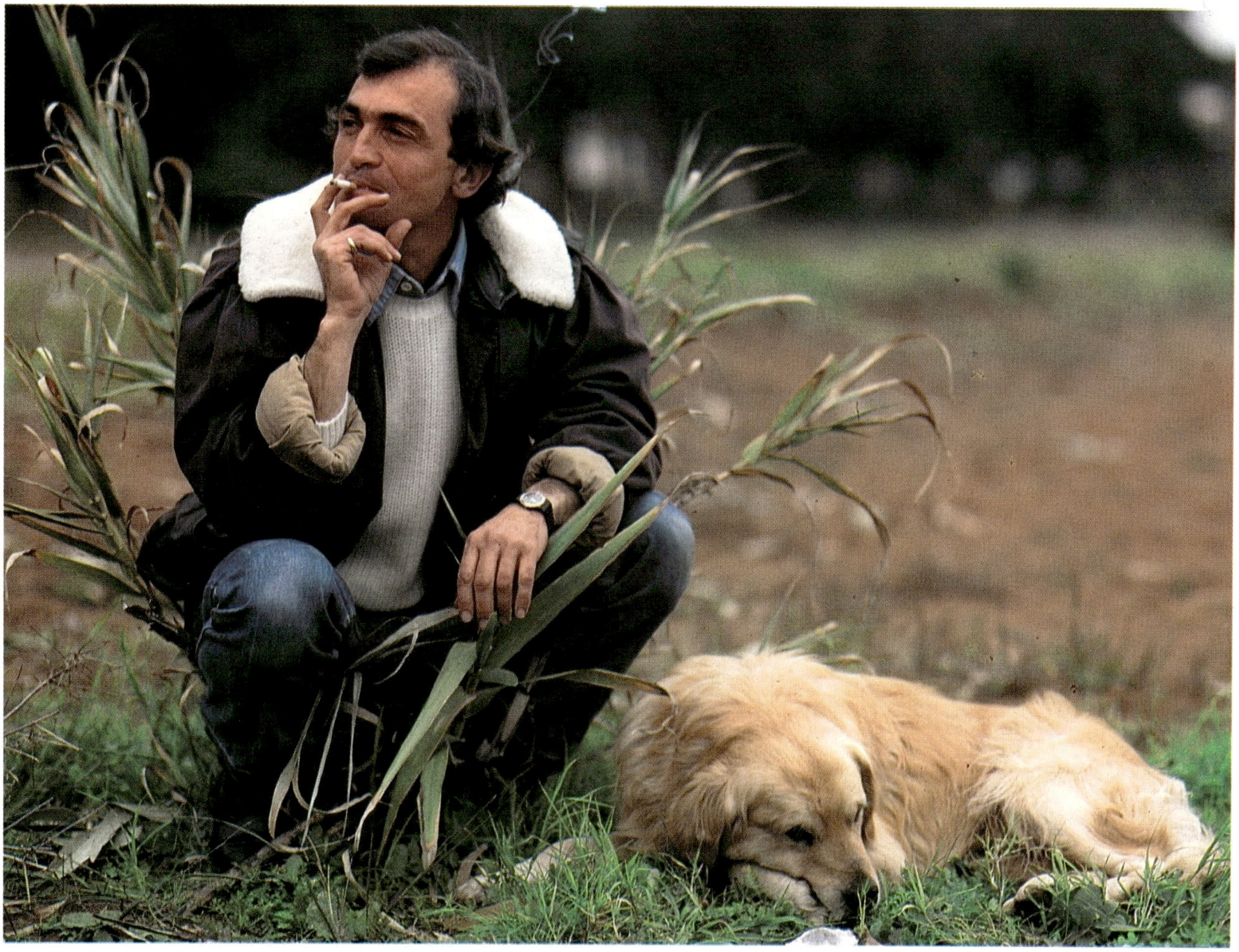

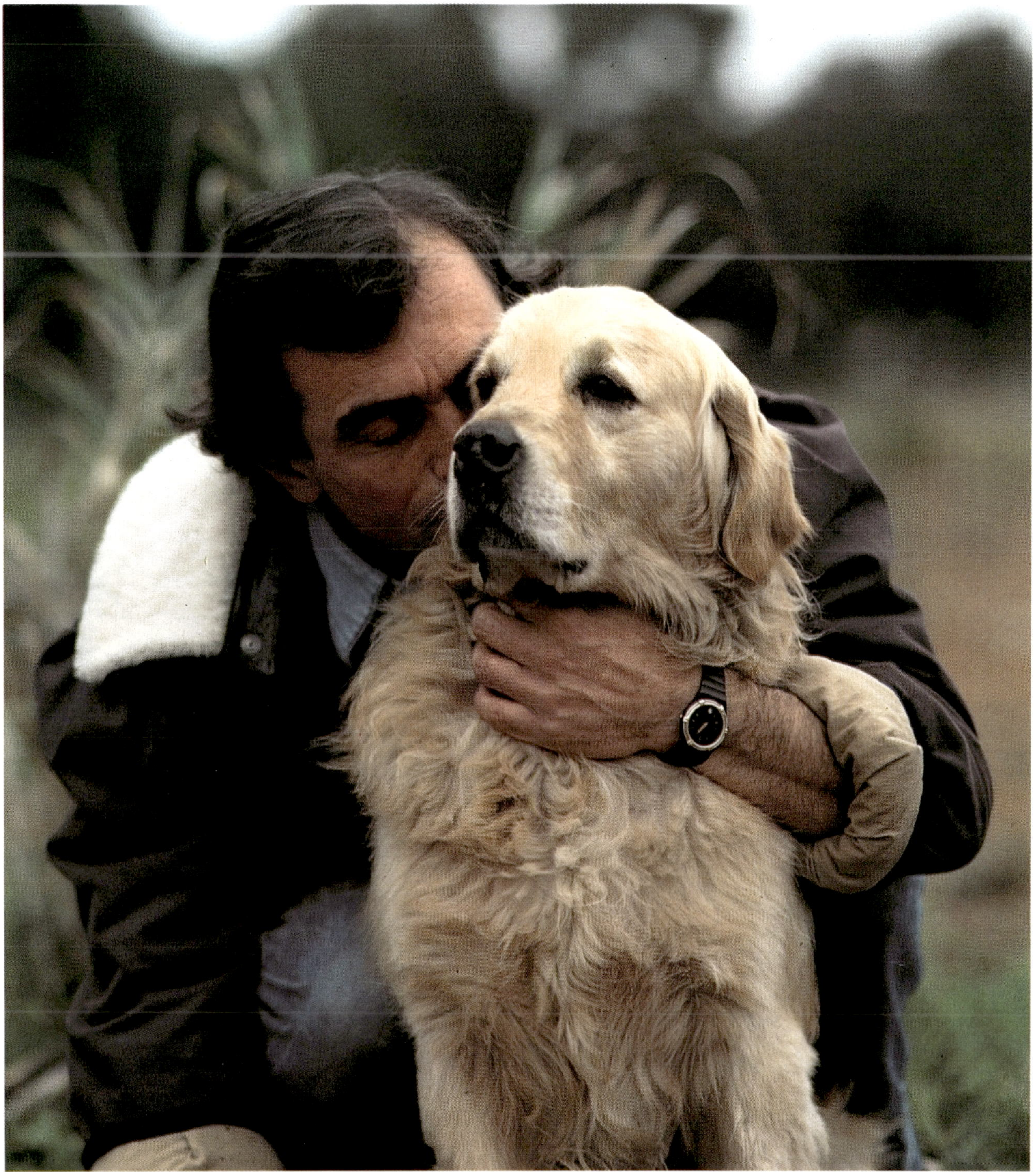

I ... simply ... adore
This young man and his labrador

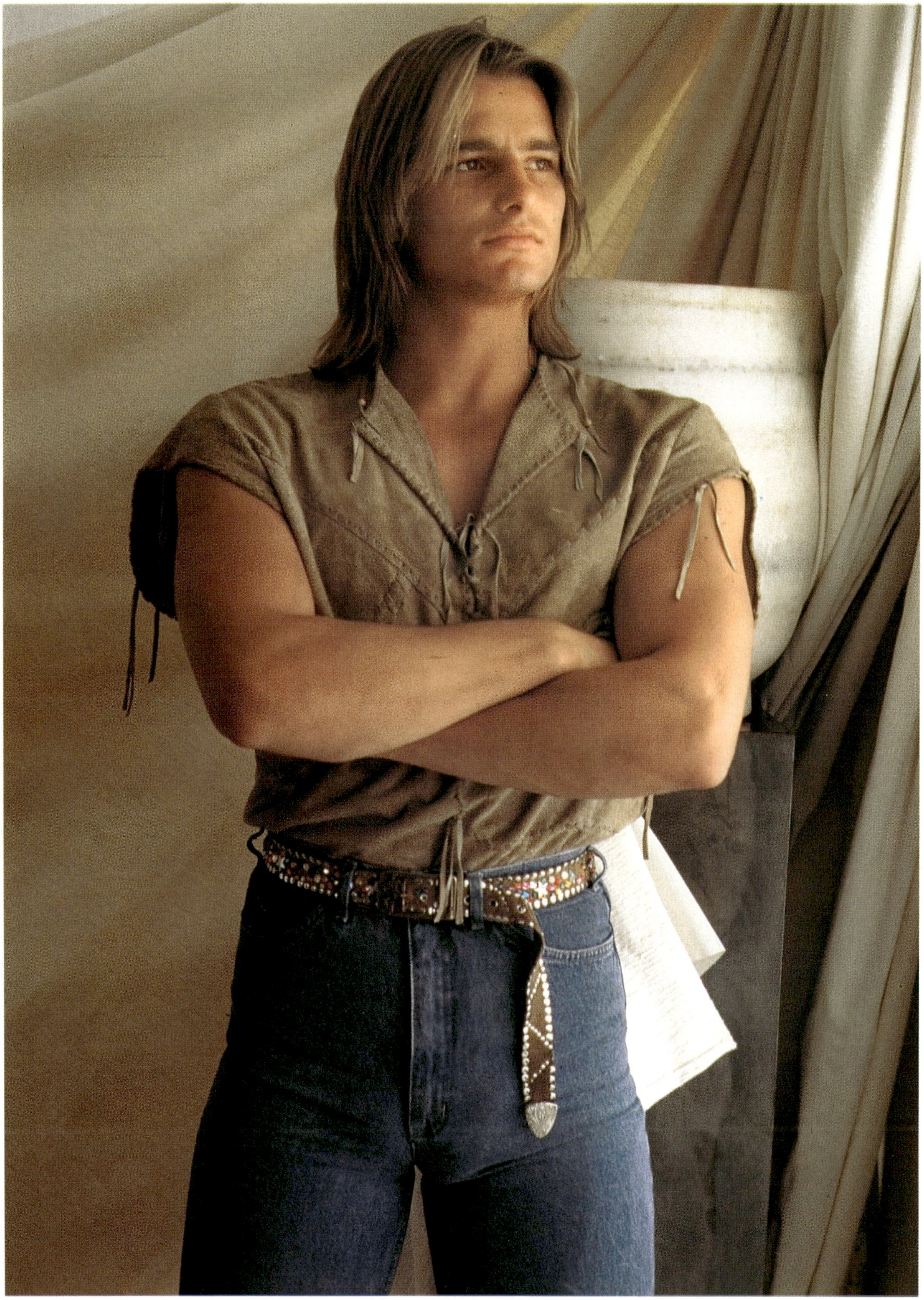

I know I've seen him once before
He certainly does look nice
And when one looks that good
... you have to show him twice

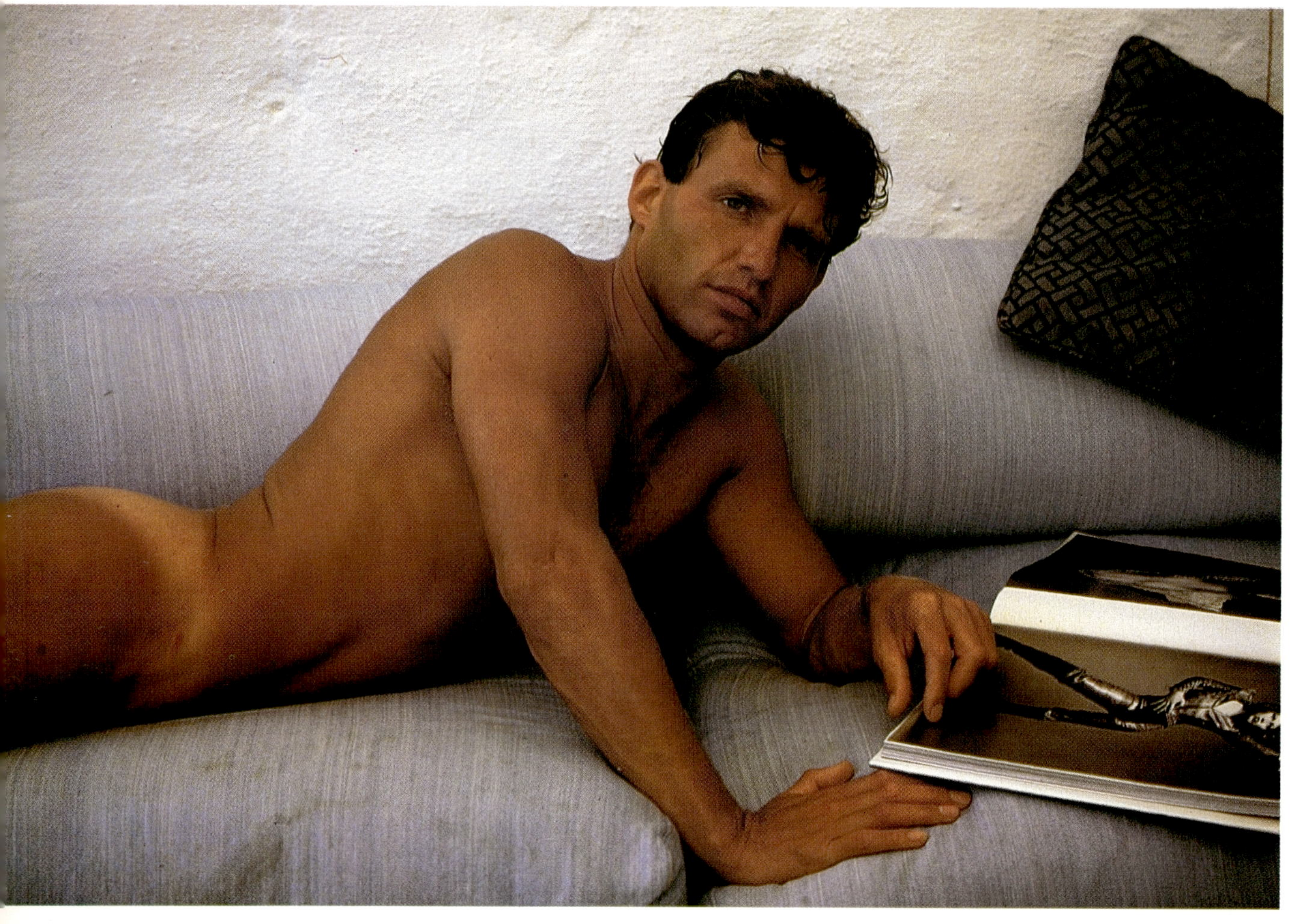

Naked and languid he lay there
Studying his book
Purely for aesthetic reasons
I thought I'd sneak a look

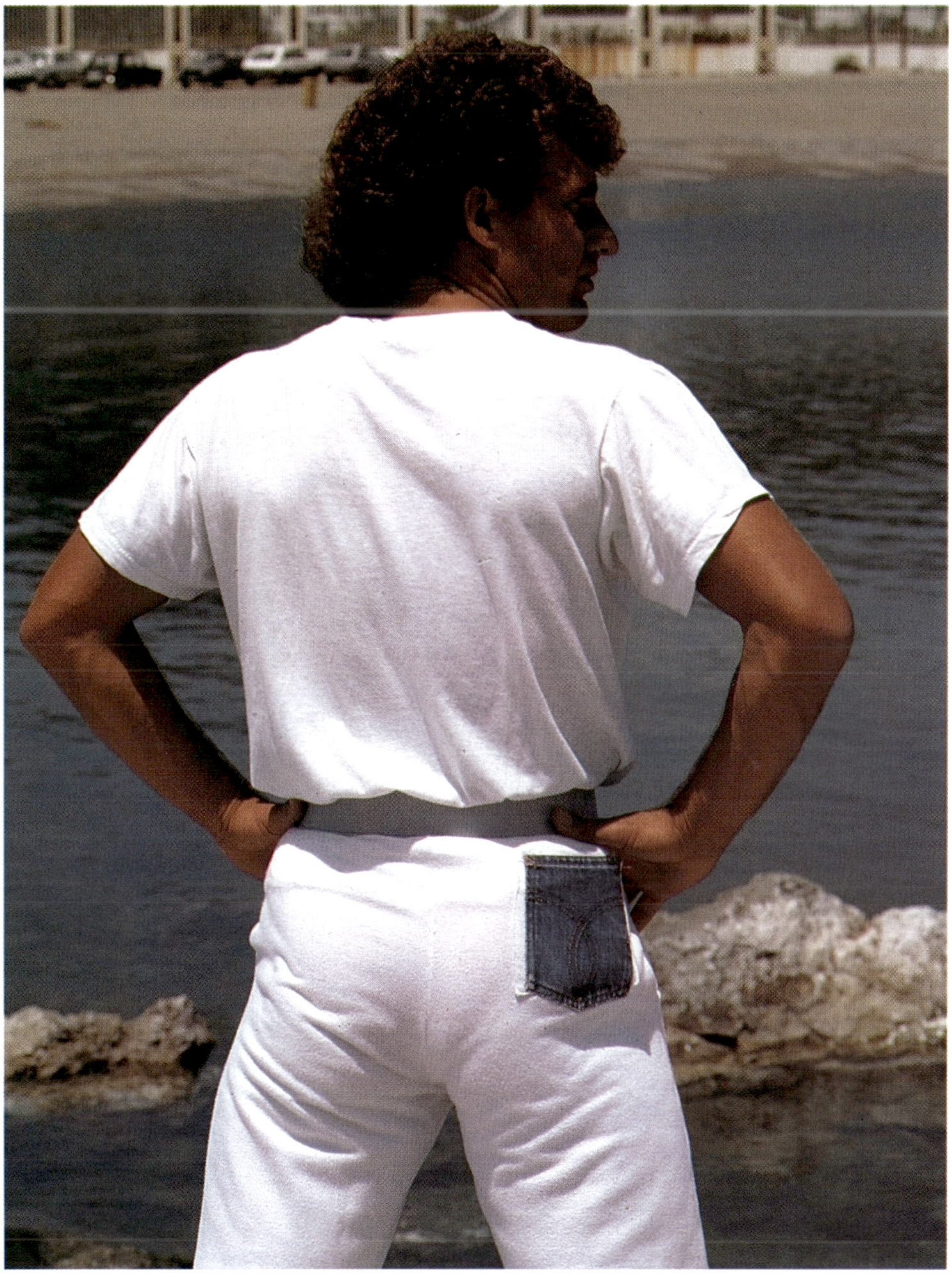

The lifeguard stood there dressed in white
Protecting everyone in sight
I wondered if he'd be all right
Those trousers looked a little tight

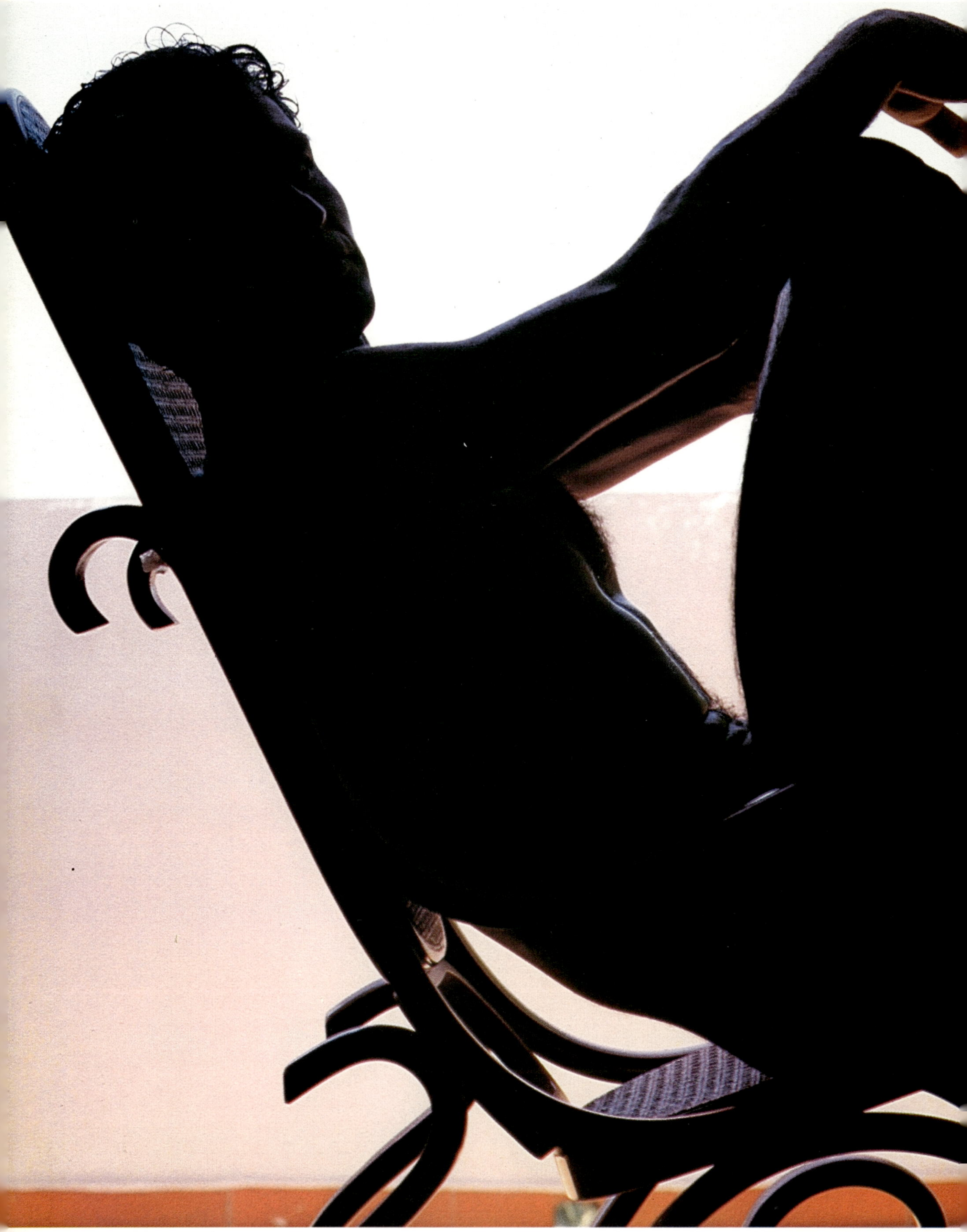

He sat there in naked repose
A nice young man without his clothes
Just what is a girl to do?
I knew it wouldn't be adieu

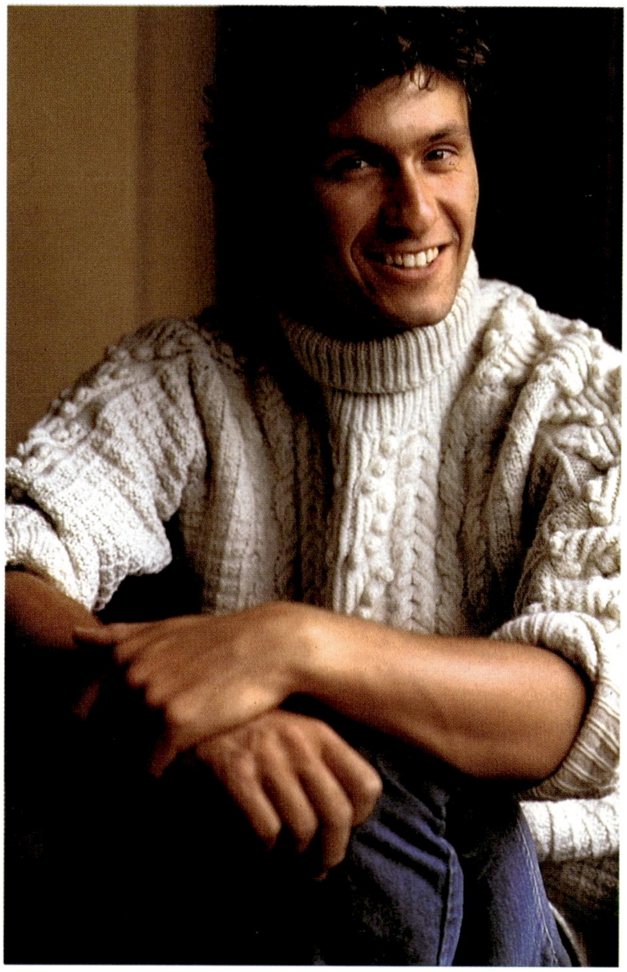

He looks a nice boy in his sweater
A little like the boy next door …
Who could ask for better?

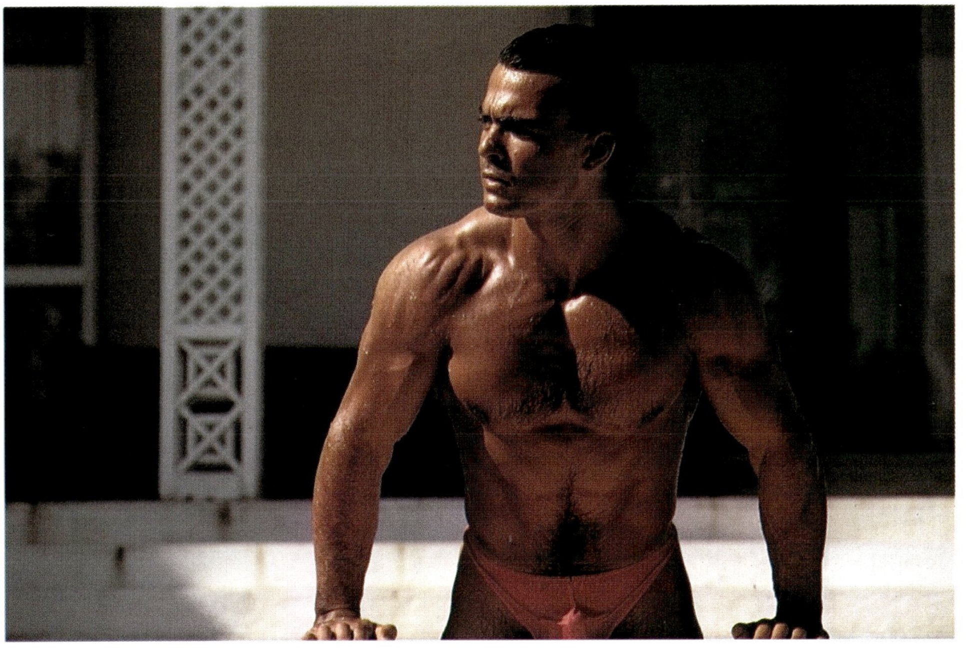

He sunned himself by the pool
Not a single word was said
He looks so tanned and super-cool
What goes on in his head?

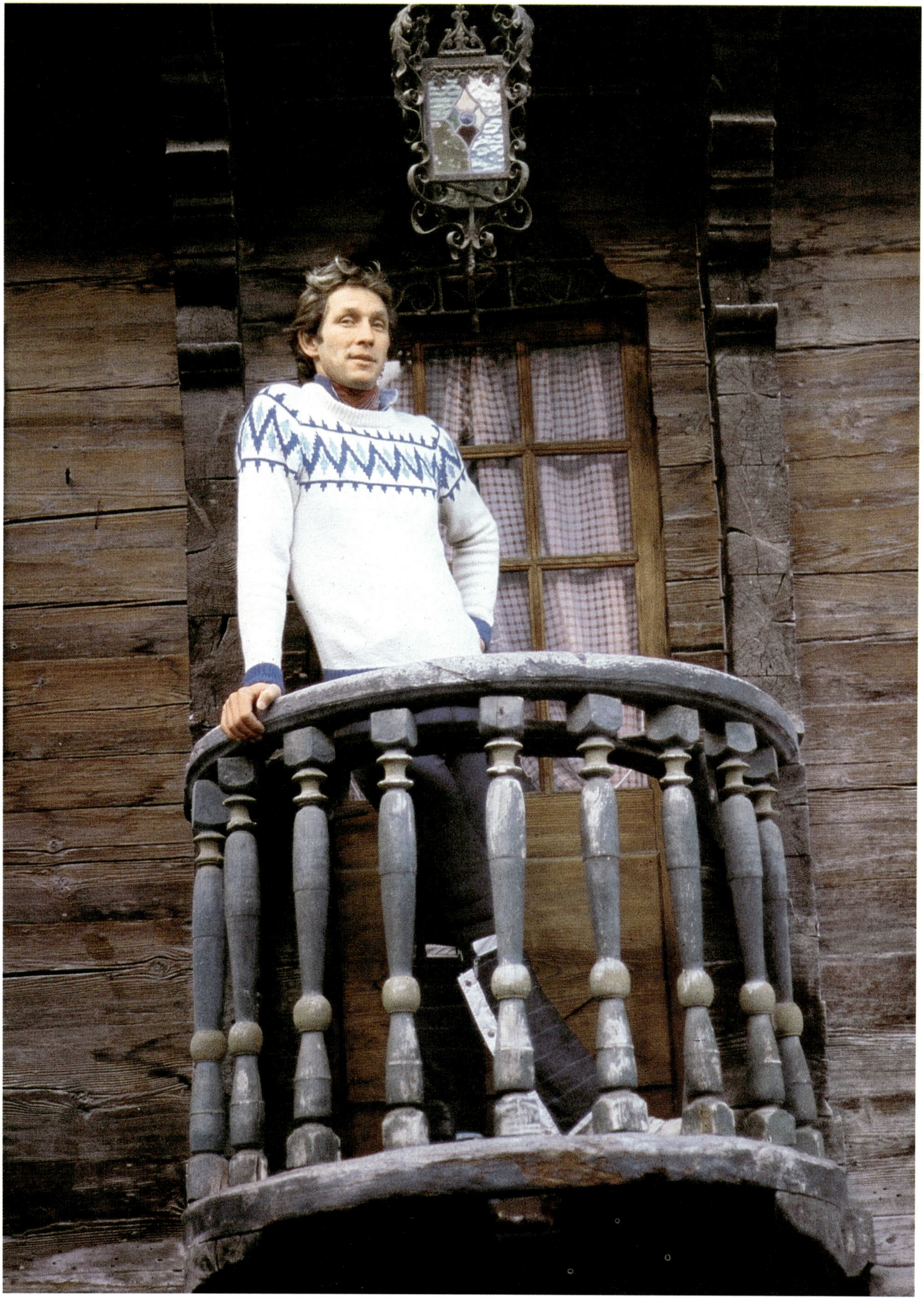

Perched up on that balcony
Striking quite a pose
Thoughts of Shakespeare came to me
I wonder if this young man knows
Juliets stand on balconies
... not their Romeos

As he sat there for a while
The light streamed in and lit his smile
Money, class, panache and style
Yuppie with a yapping puppy

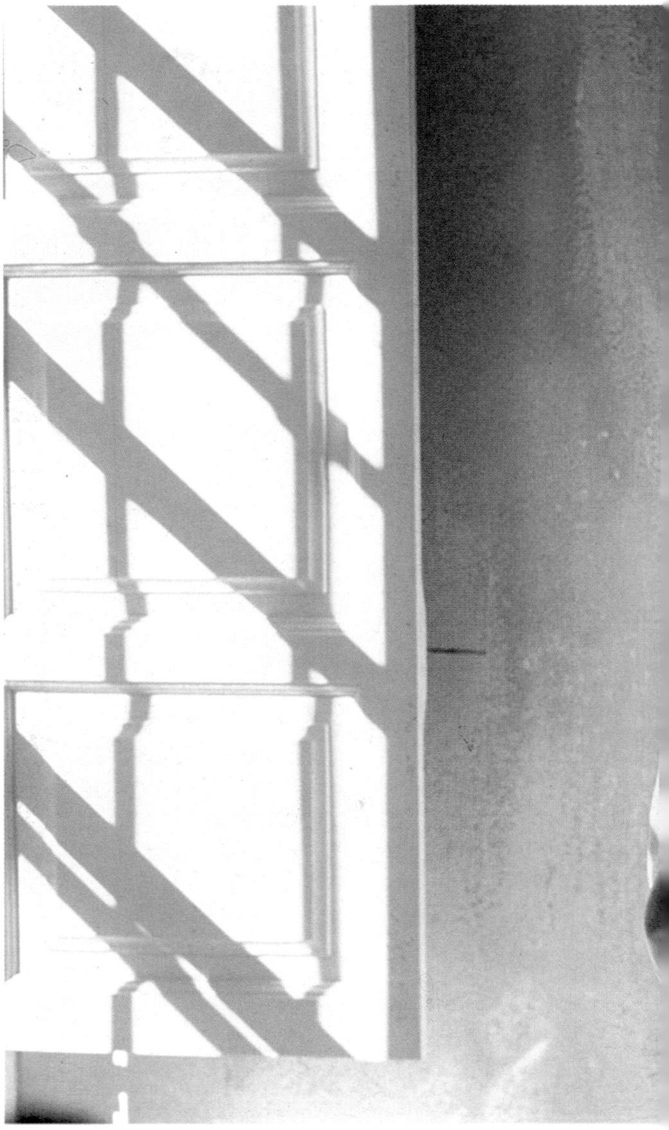

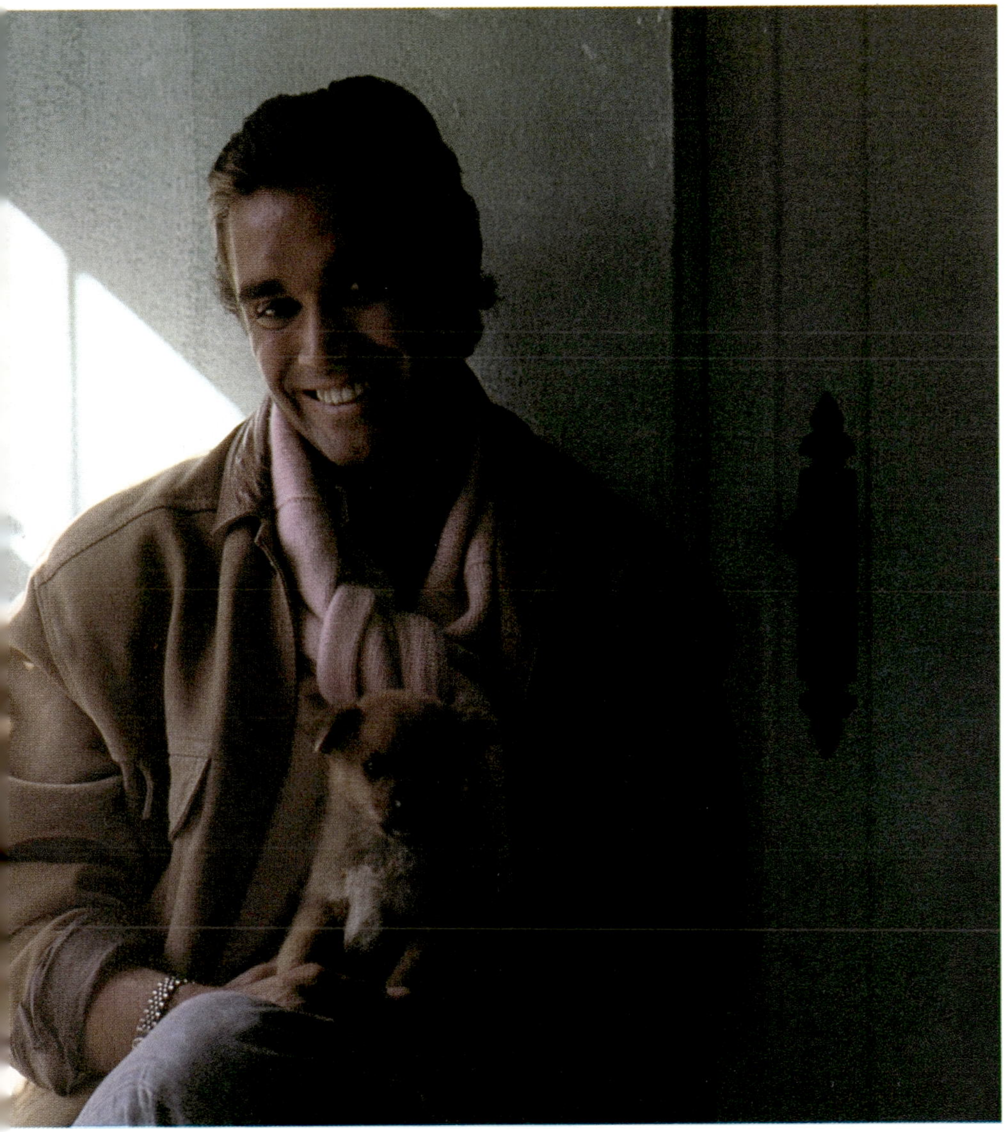

Alone the youth was sitting there
Sunlight gleaming on blond hair
As he sat astride his bike
He asked me if a ride I'd like ...
But how could it be advisable
To go off on his motorcycle?

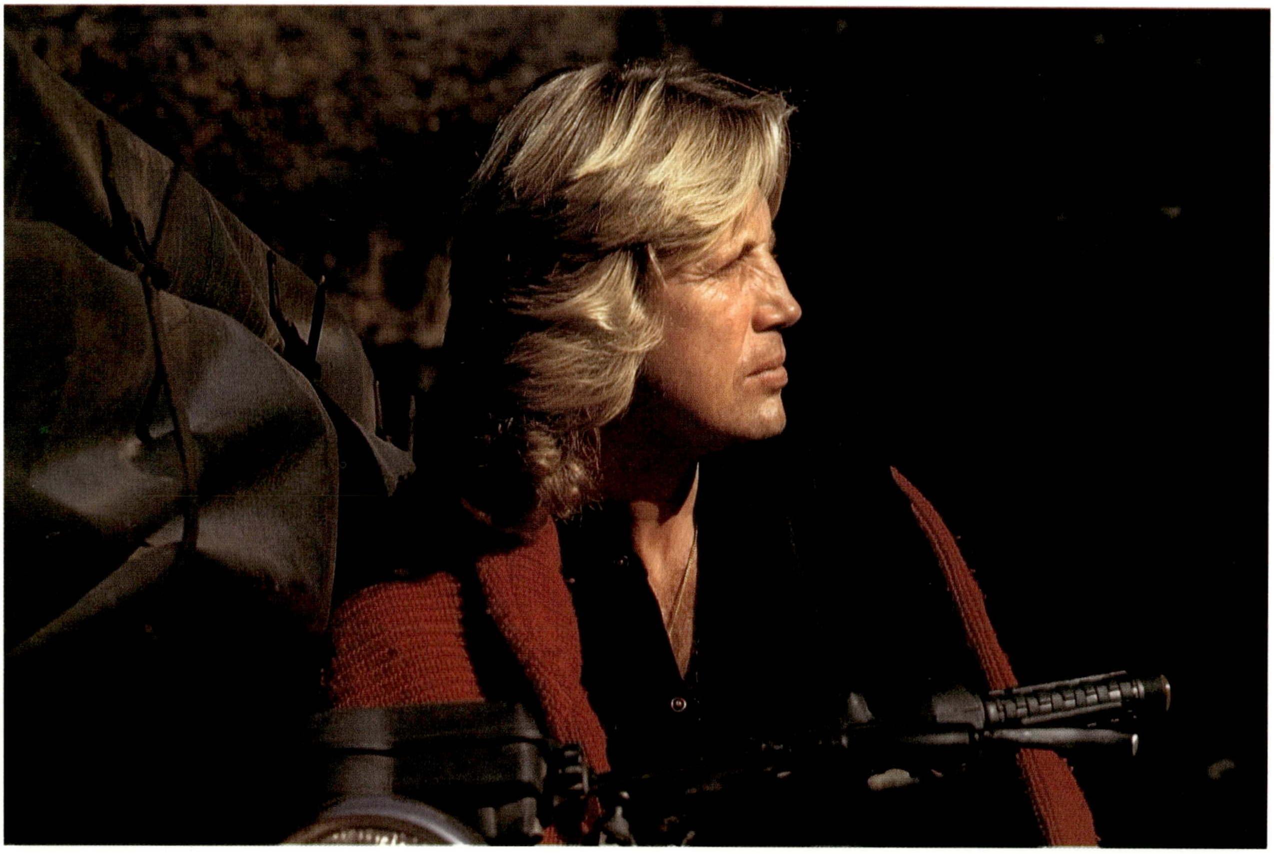

The swimmer didn't falter
As he cut right through the water
His overarm caught my eye
He did a nifty butterfly
Perhaps I'll give him a try
... but first make sure he's dry

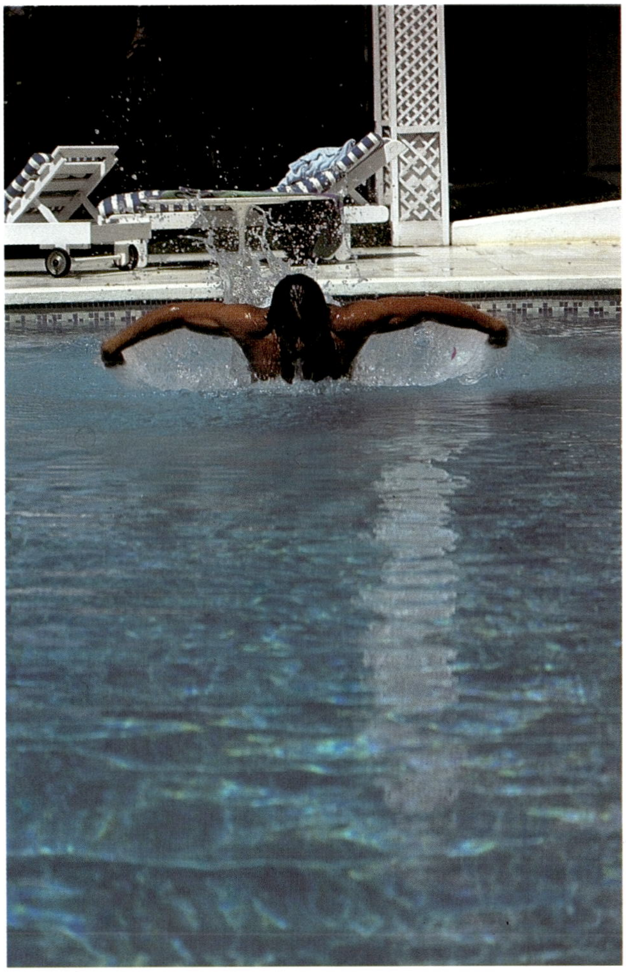

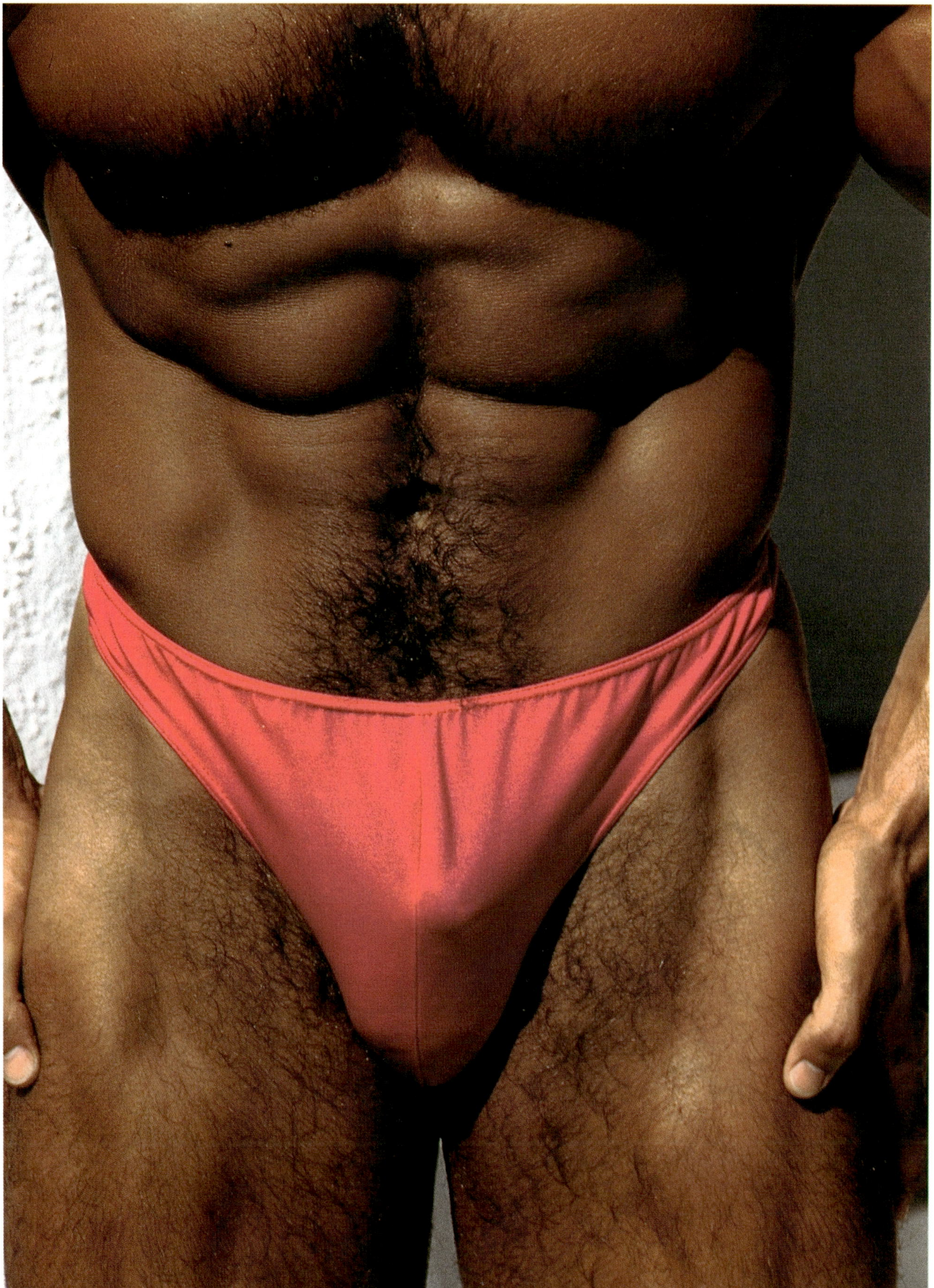

Isn't he magnificent?
One of those handsome hunks
He really took my breath away
In those saucy swimming trunks

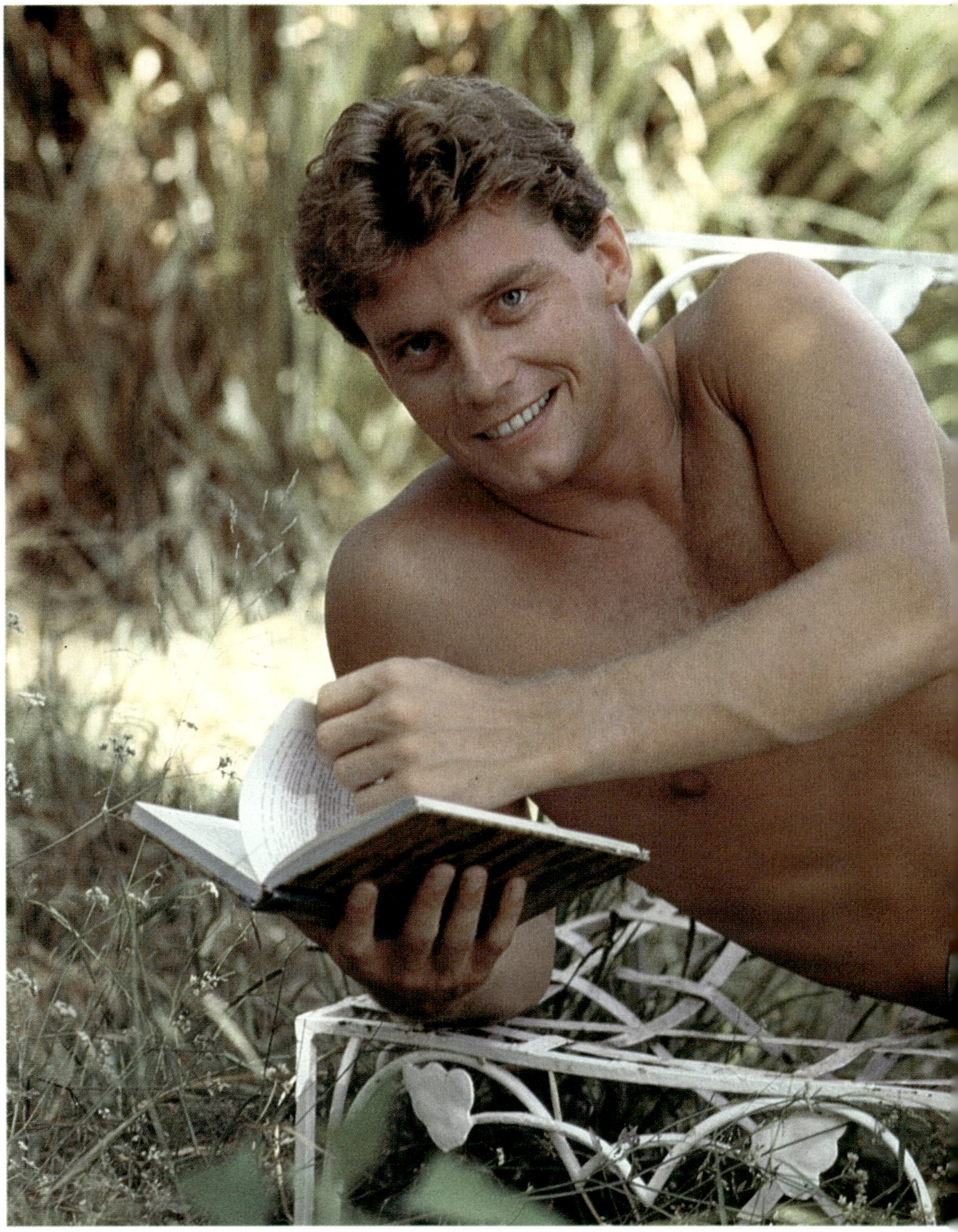

In the wild and jasmine-scented garden a young man read his book
I could tell by the twinkle in his eye and the long and lingering look
His thoughts weren't on his studies although the look was kind
It didn't take great intellect to know he had other things in mind

I glanced down at my watch as he looked across at me
It gently ticked a melody, the dial said half past three
He asked me to join him and stay awhile for tea
Although I had a busy day, how could I disagree?

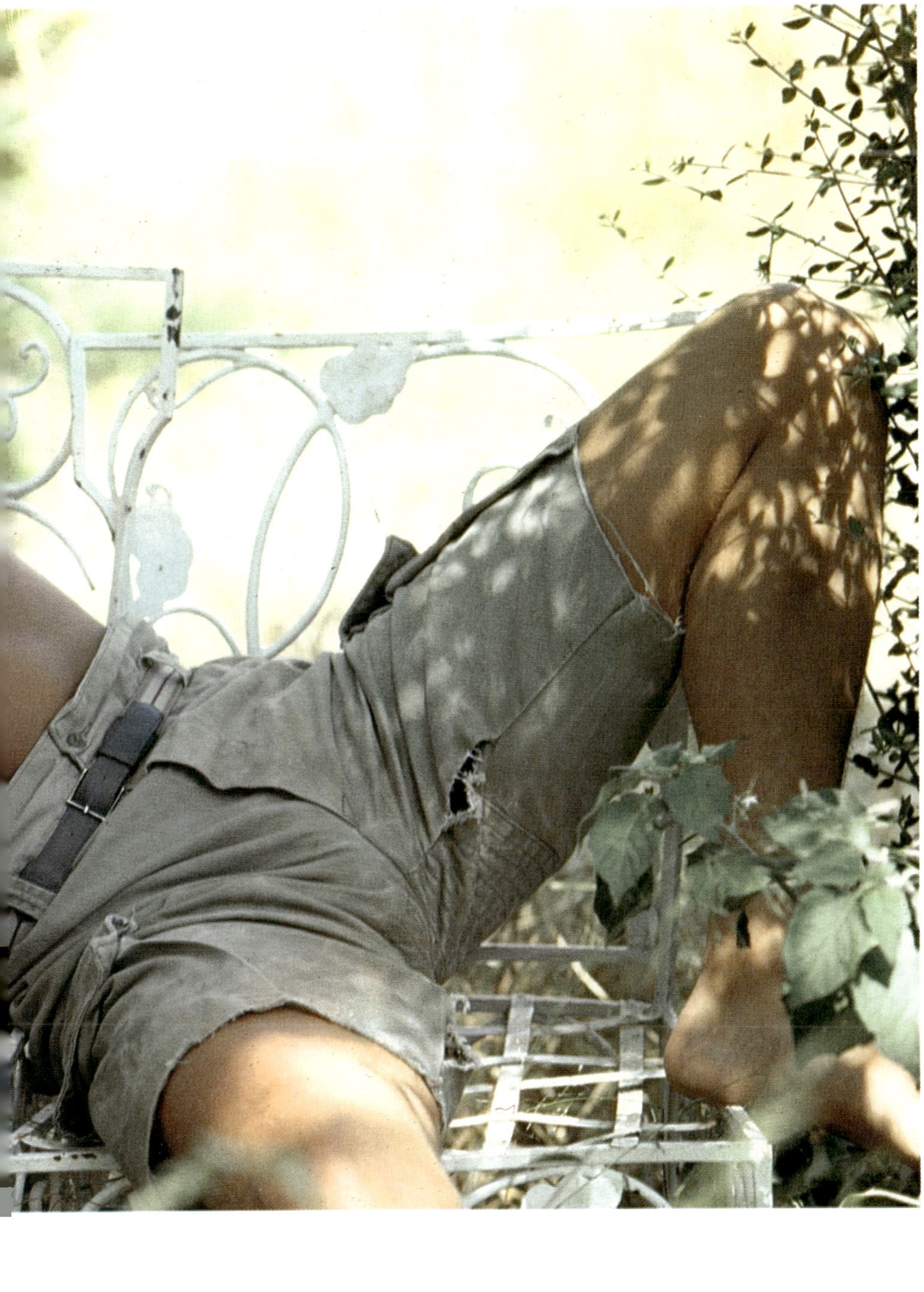

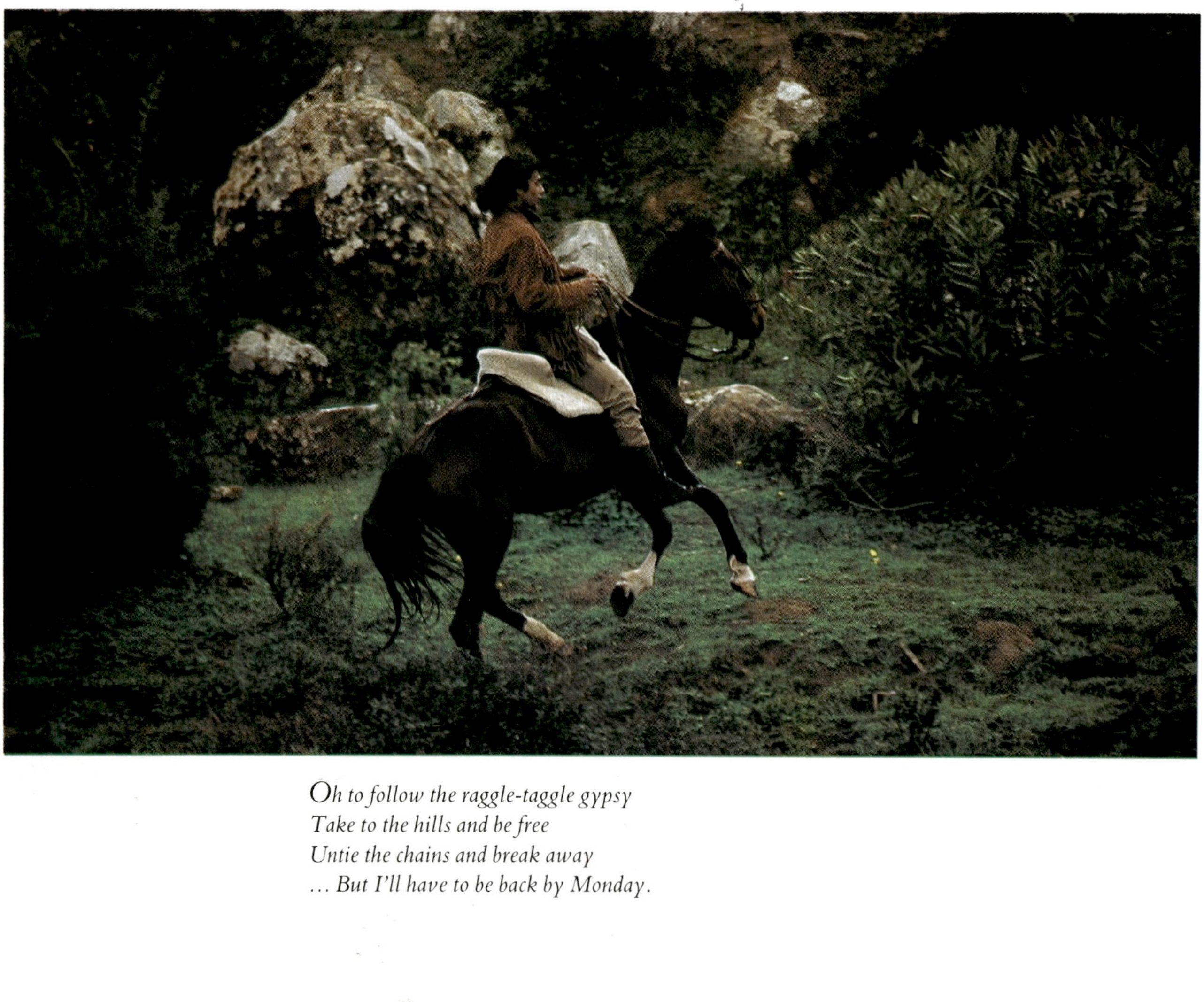

Oh to follow the raggle-taggle gypsy
Take to the hills and be free
Untie the chains and break away
… But I'll have to be back by Monday.

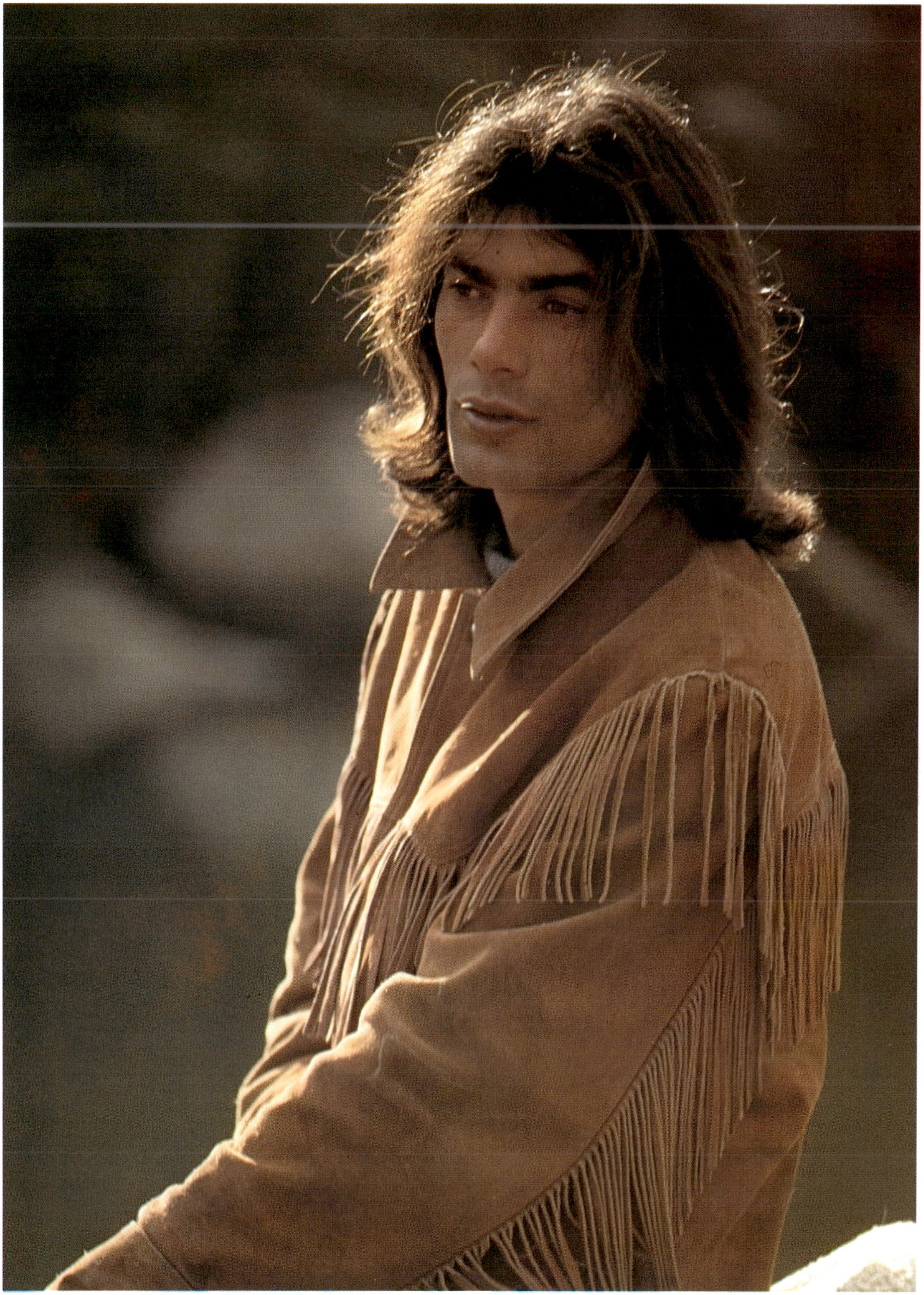

They were both knee-deep in water
The boy with the horse at his side
And I could be knee-deep in trouble
If they took me for a ride

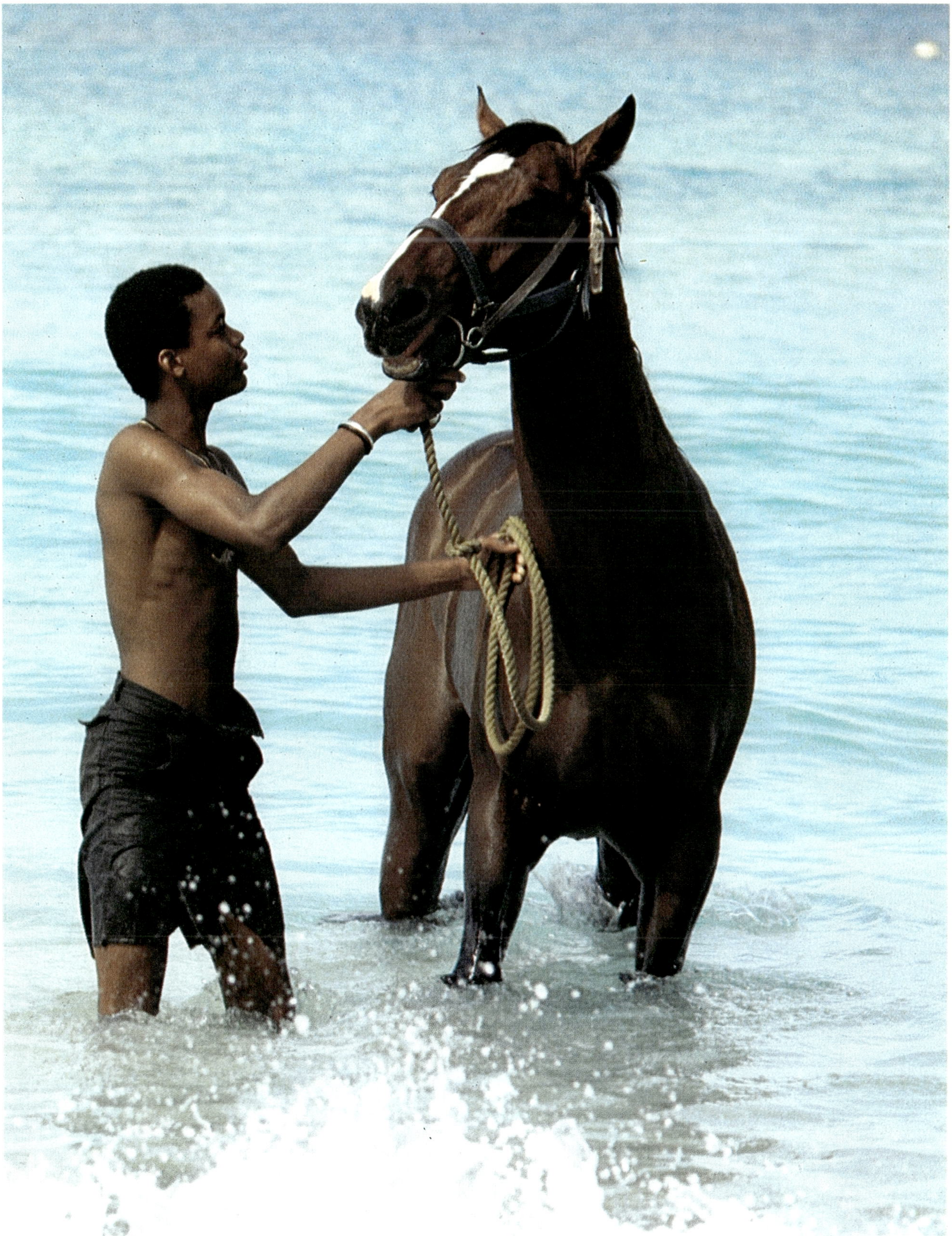

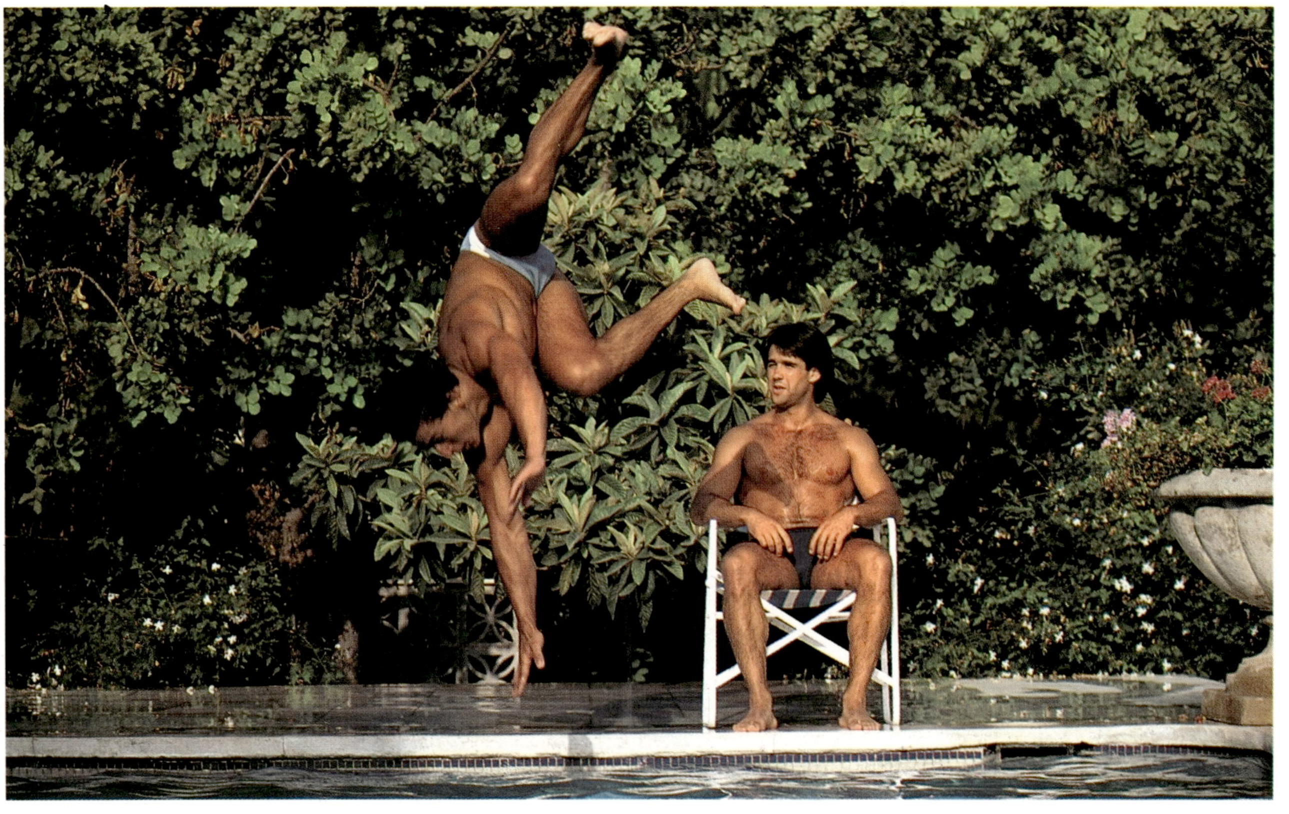

These two lads are having fun
I can't make up my mind who's to be the one
I could be getting into trouble
... Oh well, let's make that trouble double

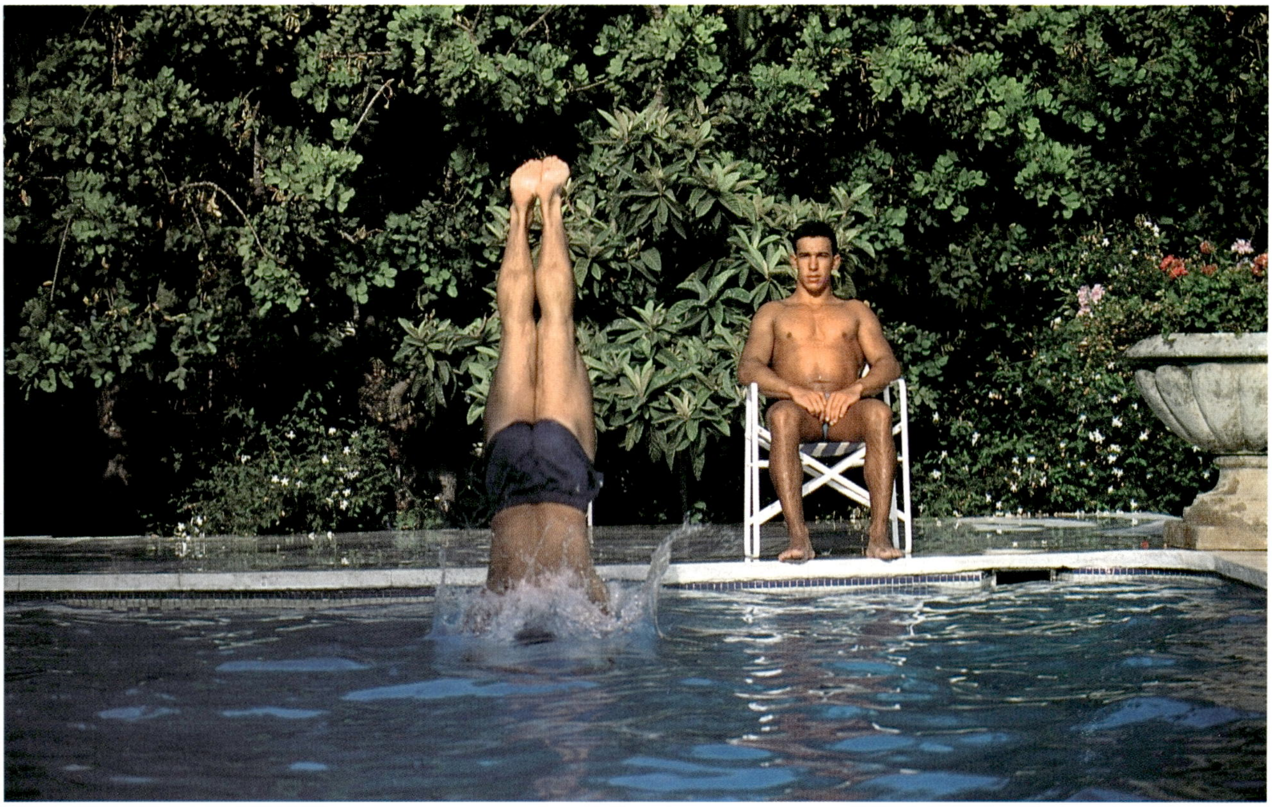

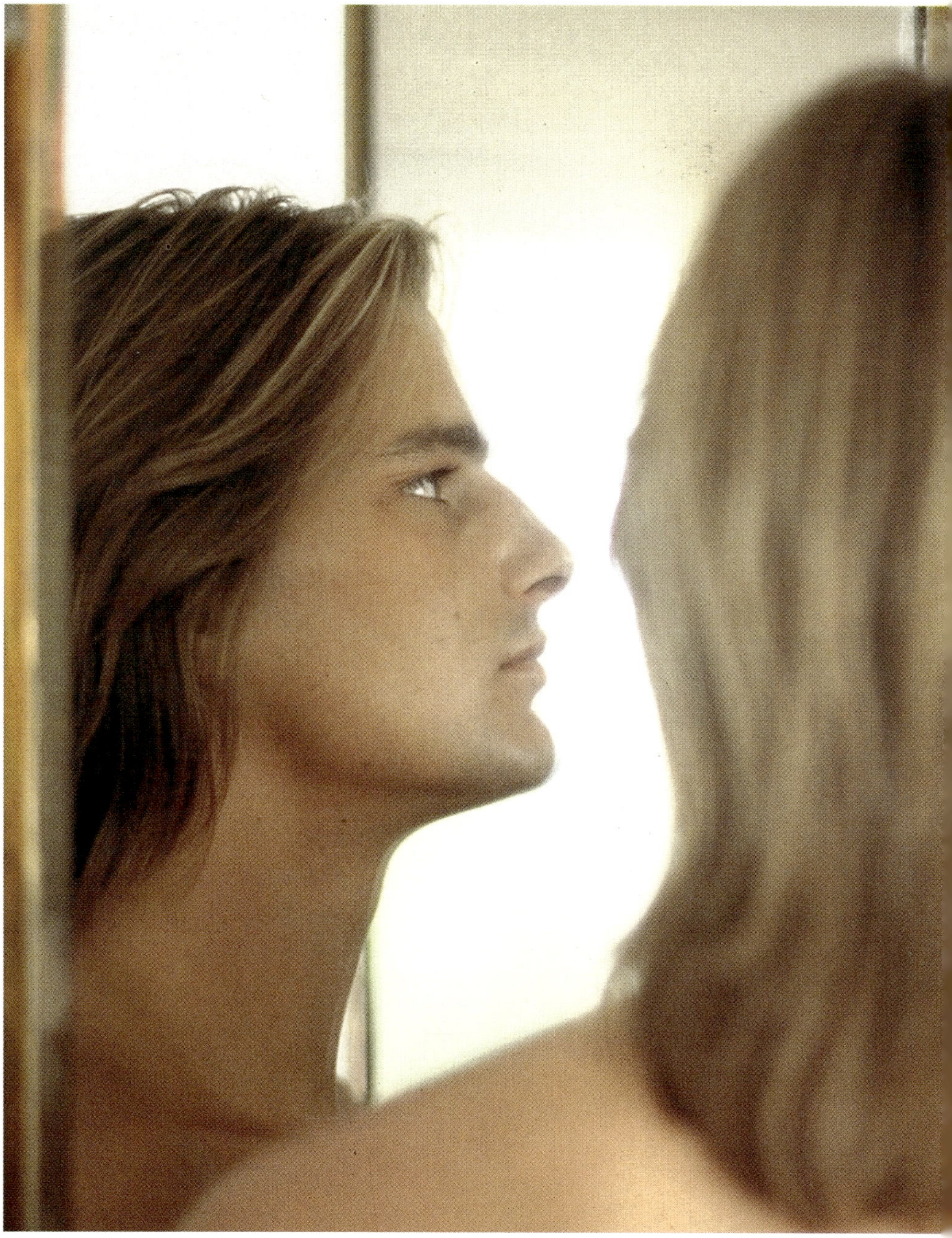

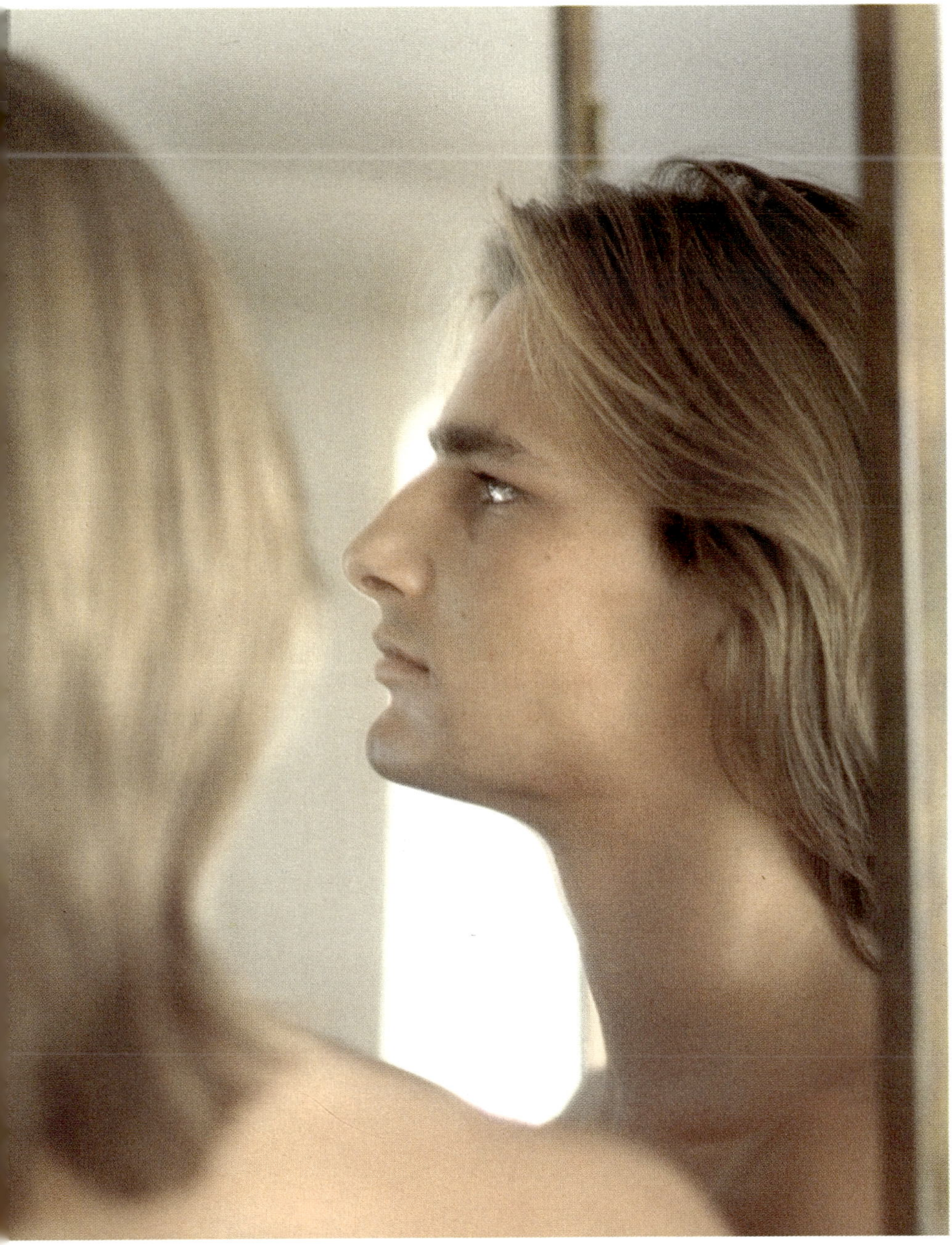

The young man gazed into the mirror
It appeared that there were three
Young men of great beauty
... But one's enough for me

It was on a magic mountain
A time I won't forget
A mystical moment
Reminiscent of Tibet
A young man contemplated
His thoughts on another plane
Transcended to another place
Somewhere ultramontane
He offered to take me with him
To this magical domain
I agreed, but on condition
We go first-class, on a plane

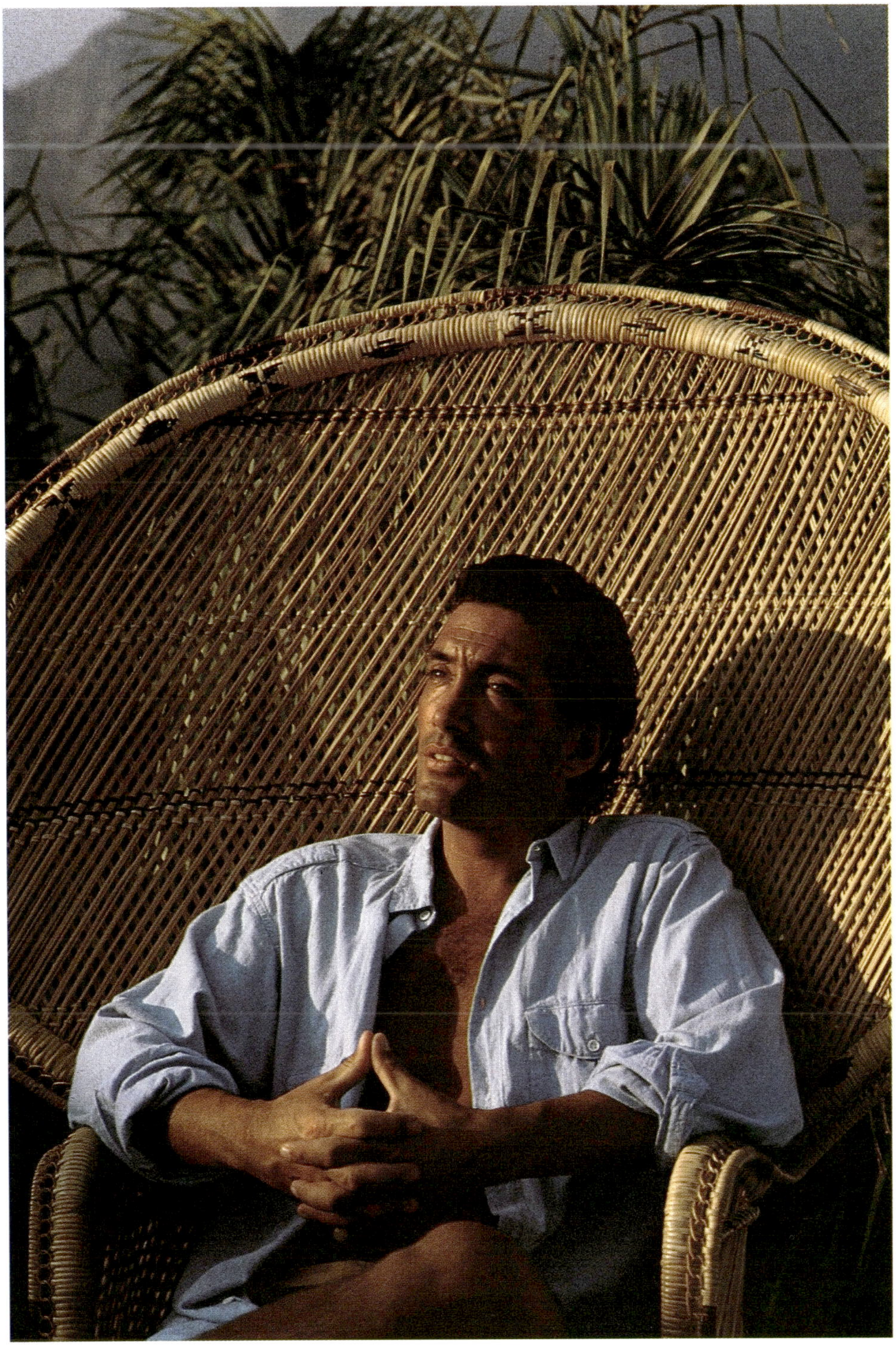

He looked very studious
With his whiskers round his throat
With pen and pencil in his hand
... will he drop me a note?

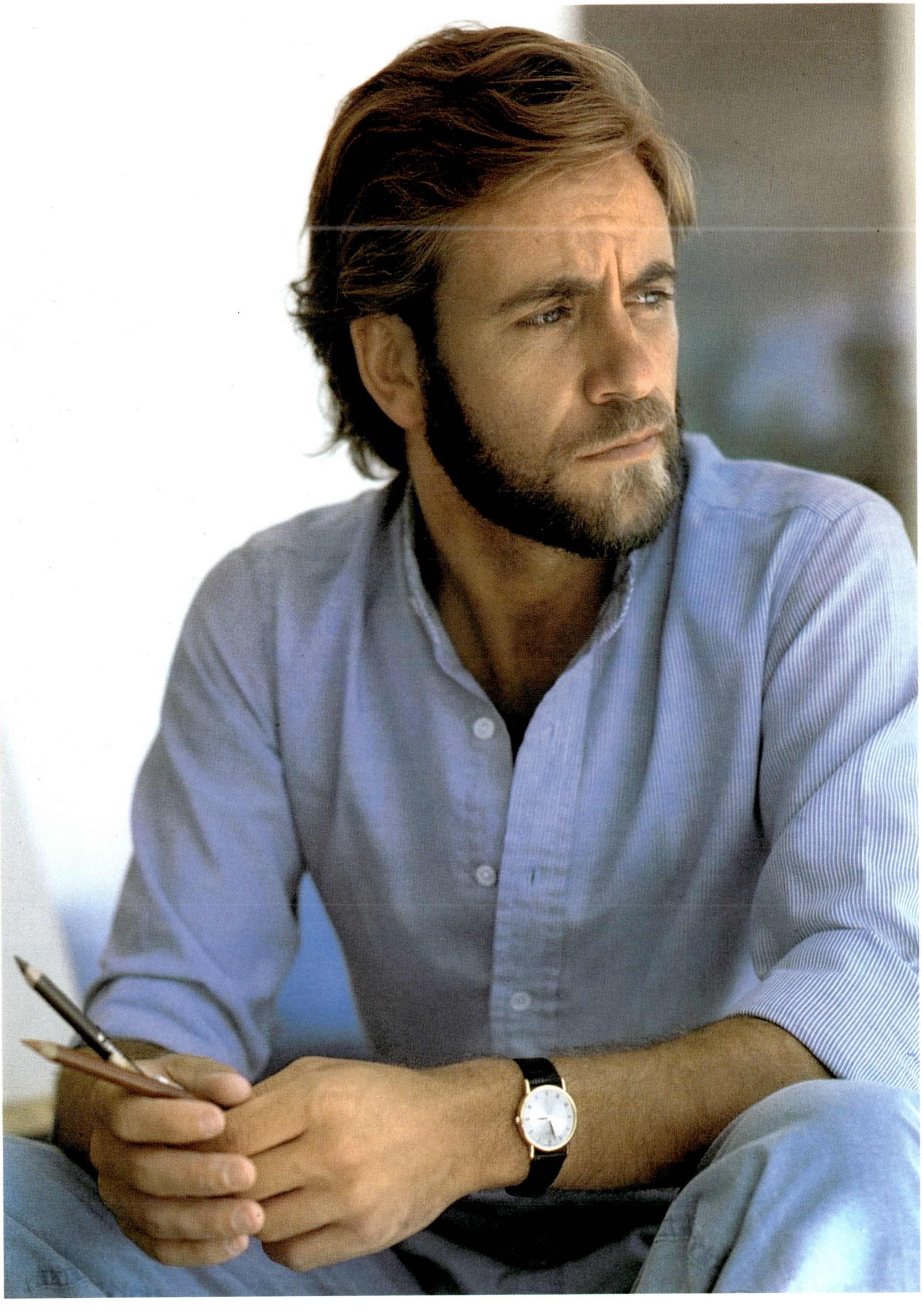

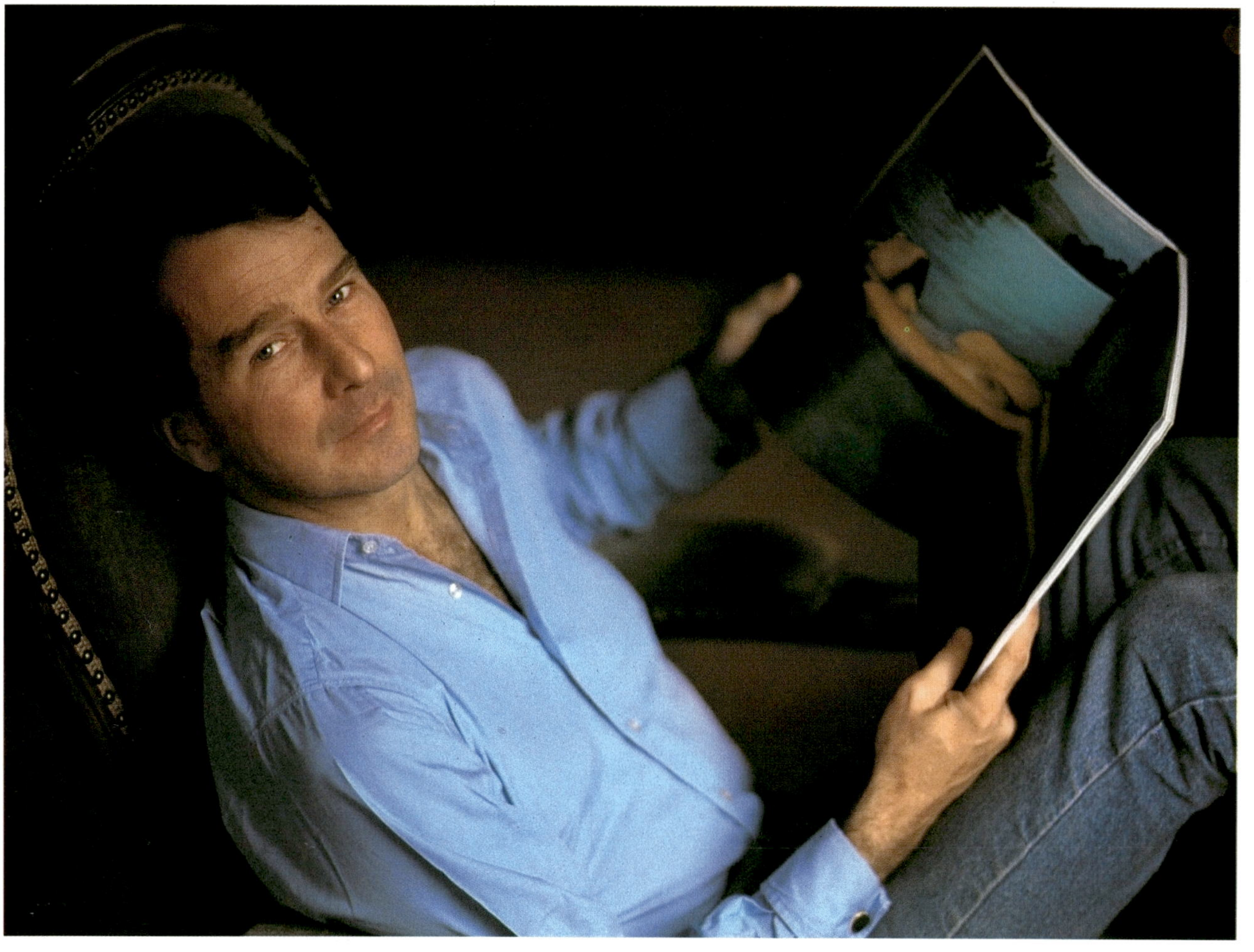

By the door the young man sat
I wonder what he's looking at?
Those pages open on his knee …
Could they be a clue for me?

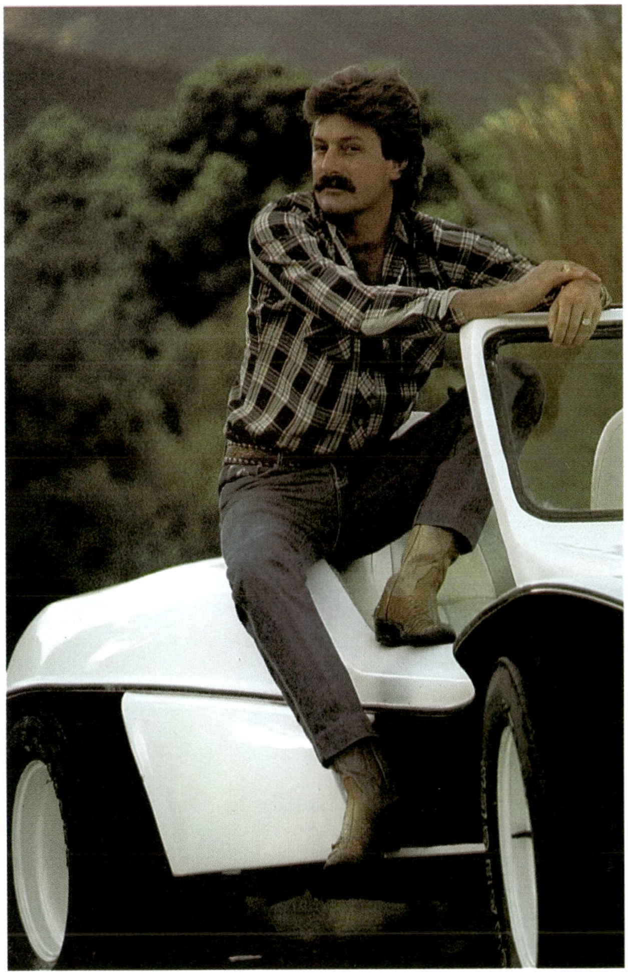

It certainly gave me a thrill
When the tall Texan rode down the hill
Just like a scene from old Rawhide
That cowboy offered to take me for a ride
But alas, romance was not to be
... I'm not squeezing into that beach buggy

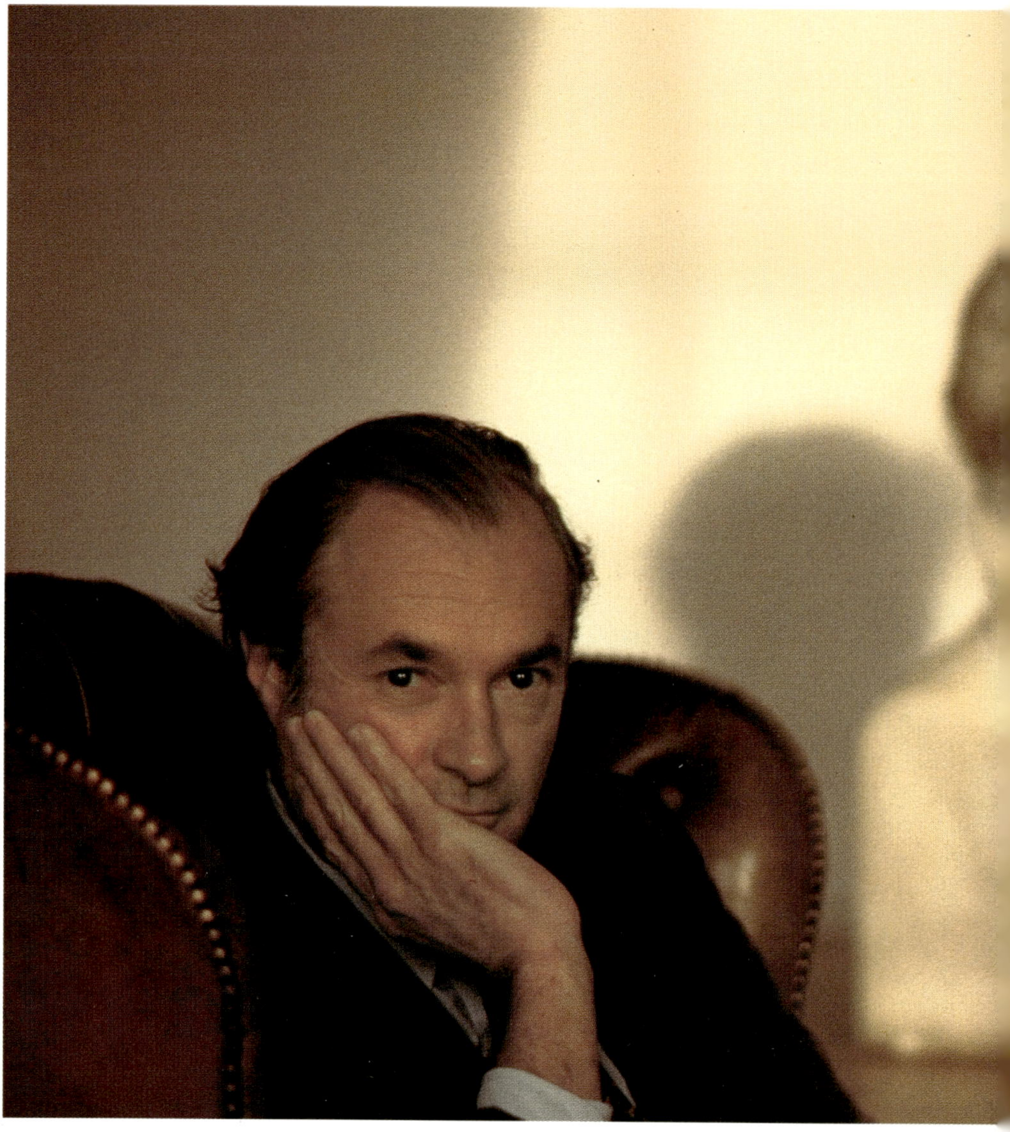

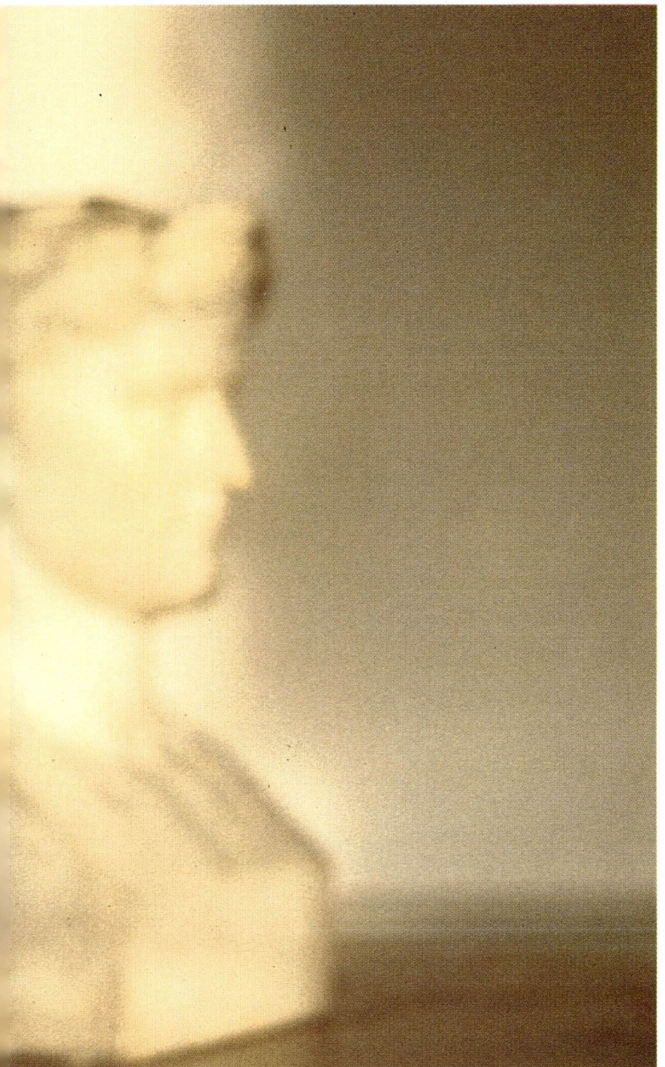

The gentleman was very moody
Contemplating in his study
In the air was a rhapsody
A melody by Vivaldi
What was in his thoughts?
Memories of distant ports?
Maybe he had a wanderlust
Inspired by a Napoleonic bust
The Kalahari, Anticosti, Tibesti,
Ashanti or Djibouti
Was he thinking of a beauty?
Hesione, Aphrodite, Amphitrite,
Rosemary Clooney?

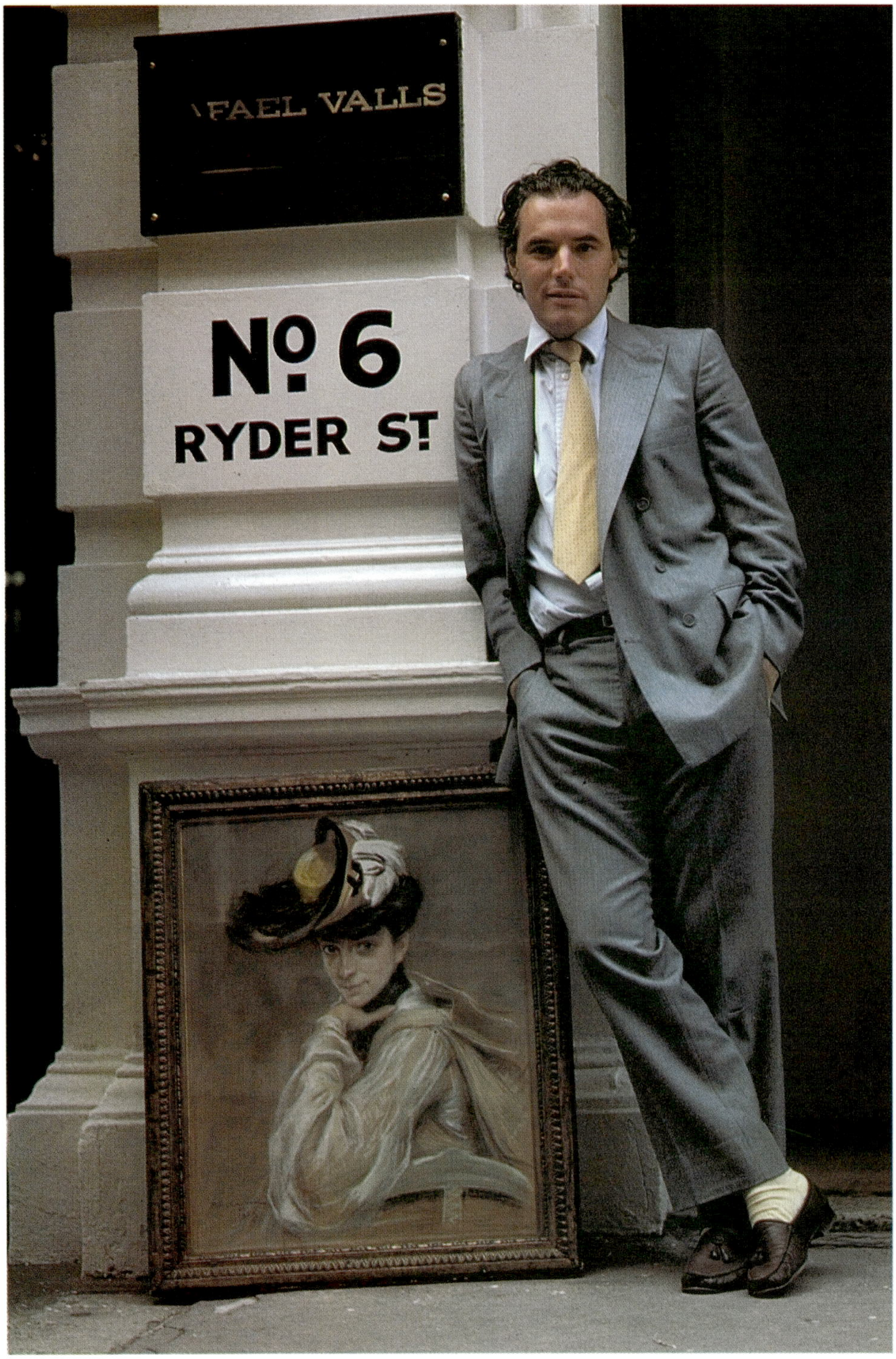
FAEL VALLS
Nº 6
RYDER ST

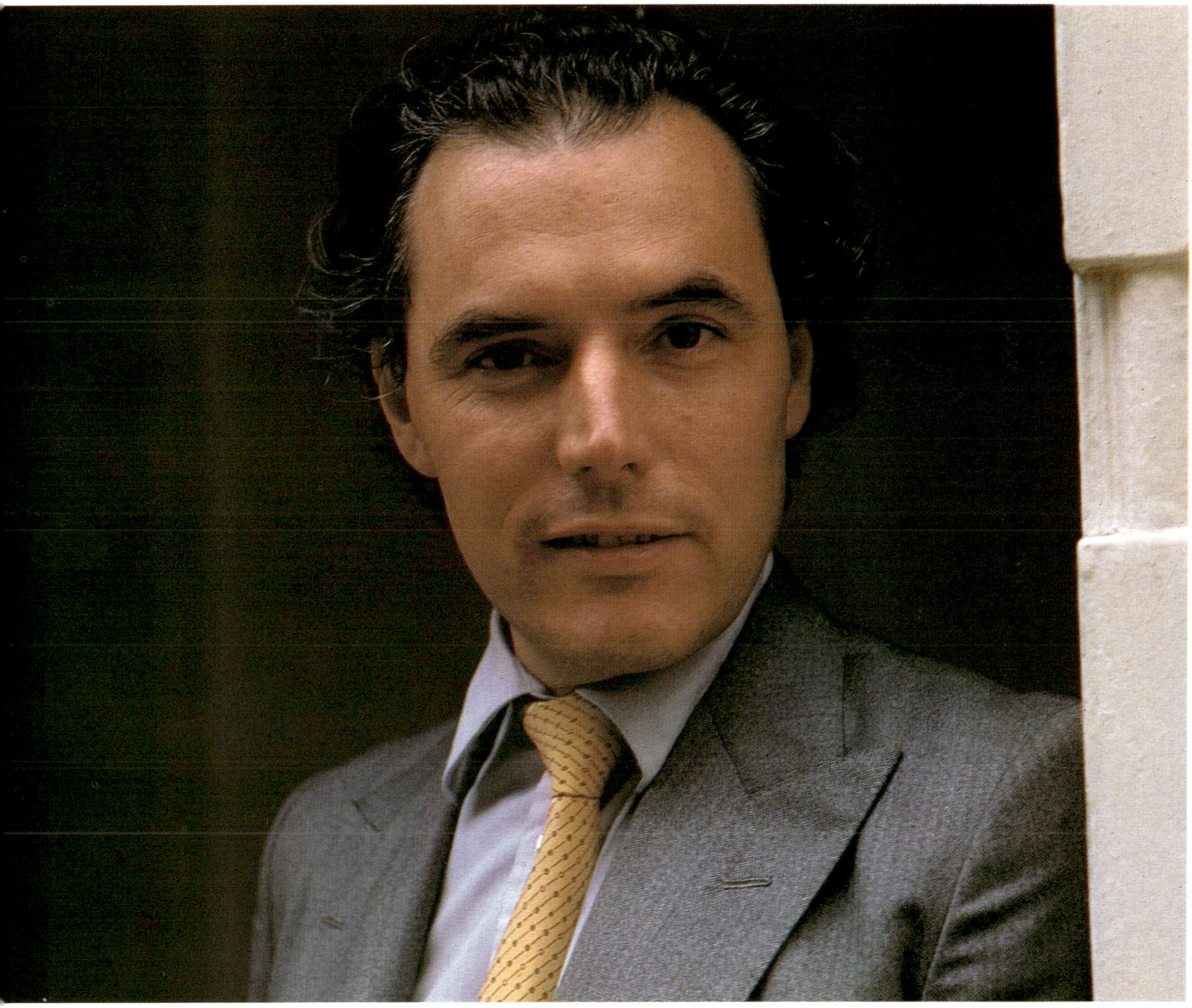

That naughty boy with a twinkle in his eye
Spoke to me as I passed by
He said he'd teach me about art,
Painting, sculpture, plays, Mozart
But he seems to me a sinner
... Maybe I'll find out after dinner

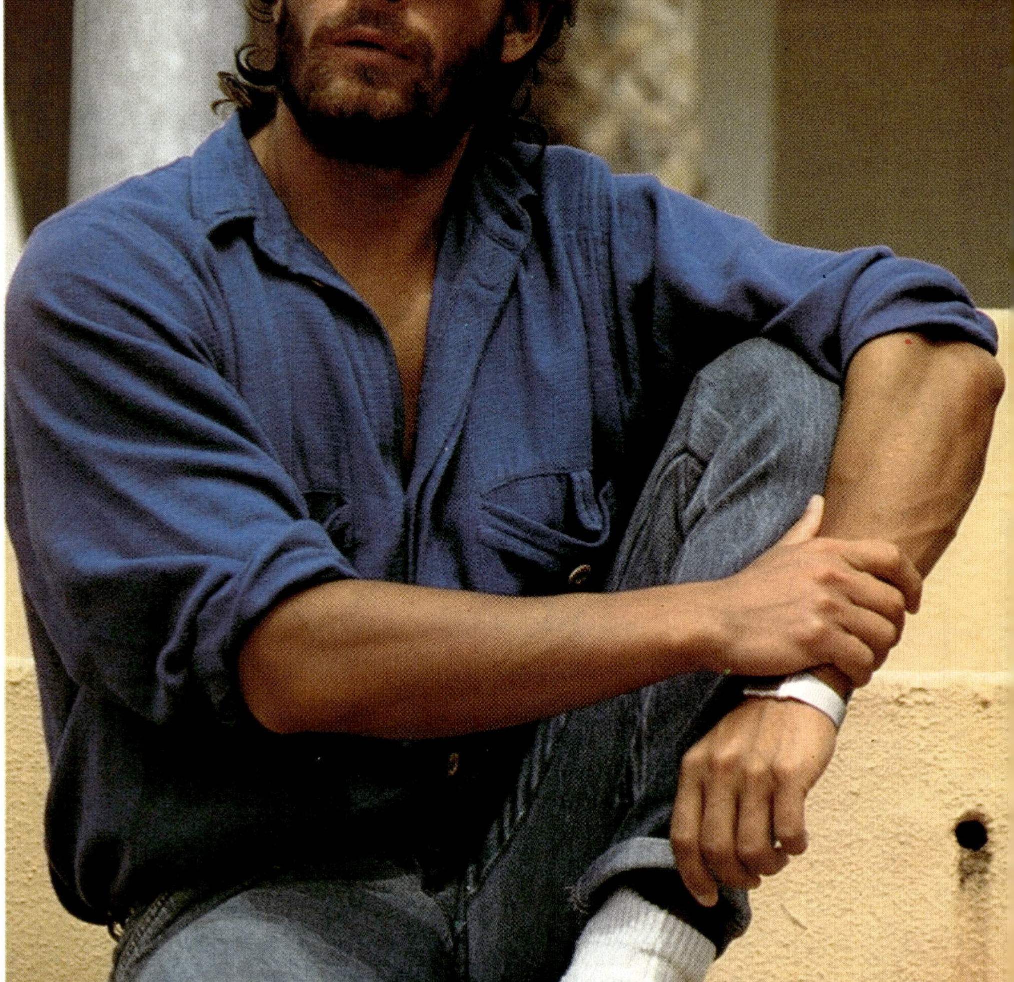

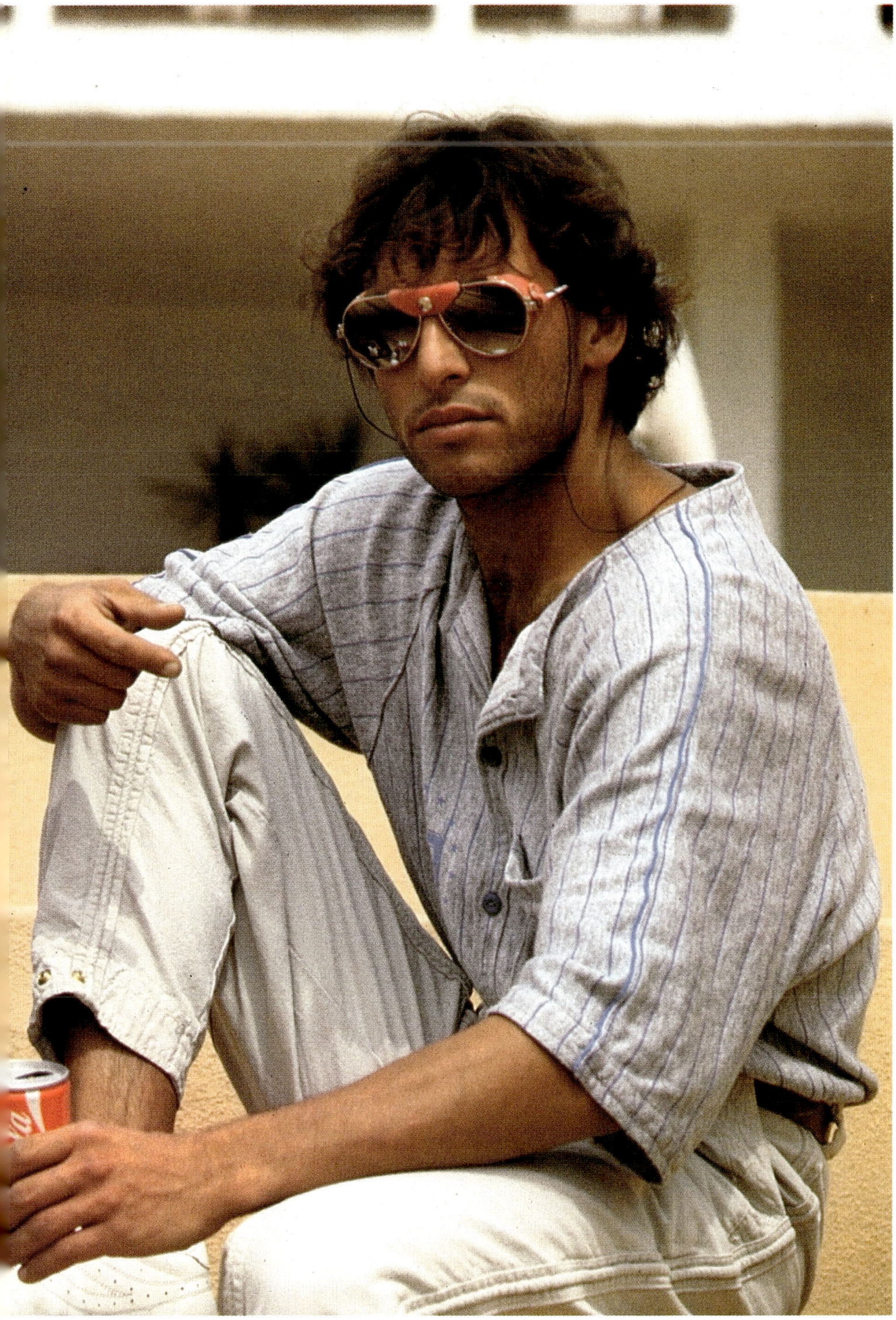

Two young and handsome guys watched by the tennis court
One could tell by their cool and shaded gaze
They liked a little sport

This driver's got a cheeky grin
Sitting in his limousine
If one took a ride inside
Would his cheekiness subside?

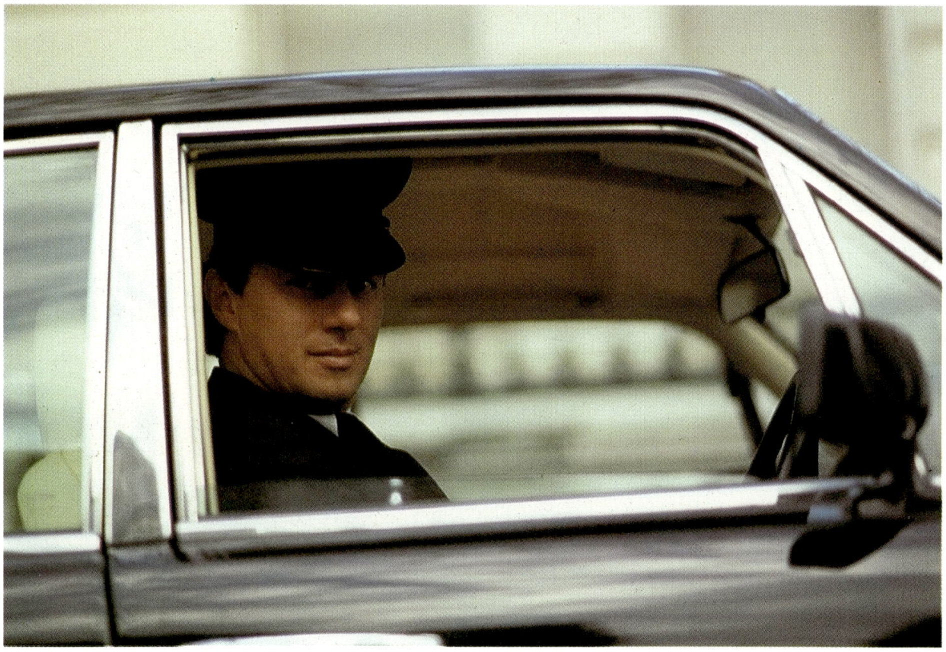

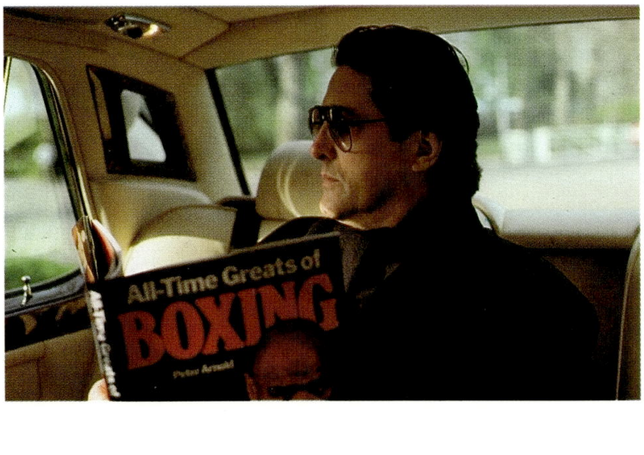

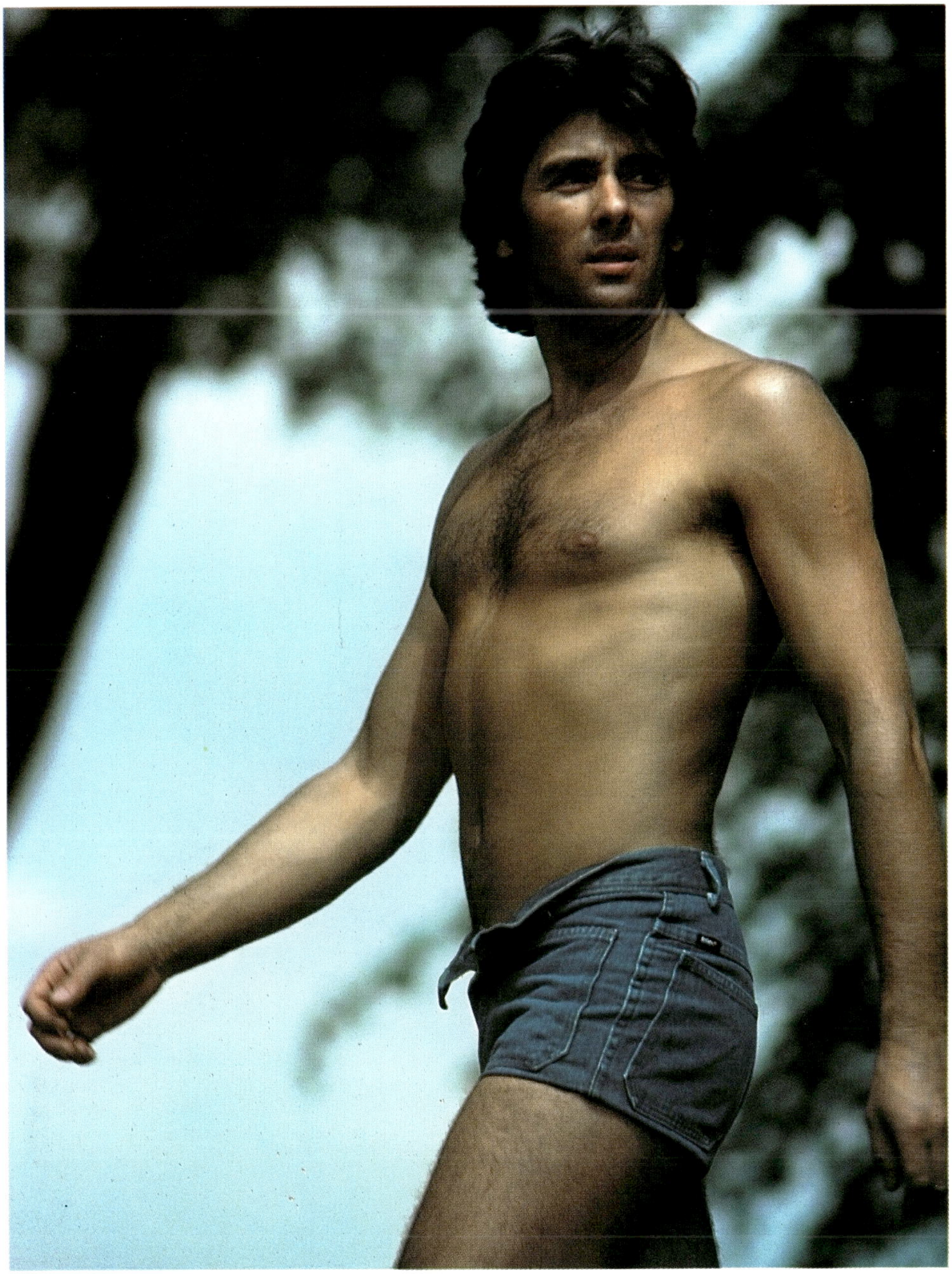

He walks the beach, a handsome chap
Looking at the girls who pass him by
Studying each one in turn
I'll show him my curriculum vitae

In the setting sun taking the air
The young man, tall and fair
In black tie and evening wear
Looked so smart and debonair
Whom will he take to the ball?
Surely we'd make a handsome pair?

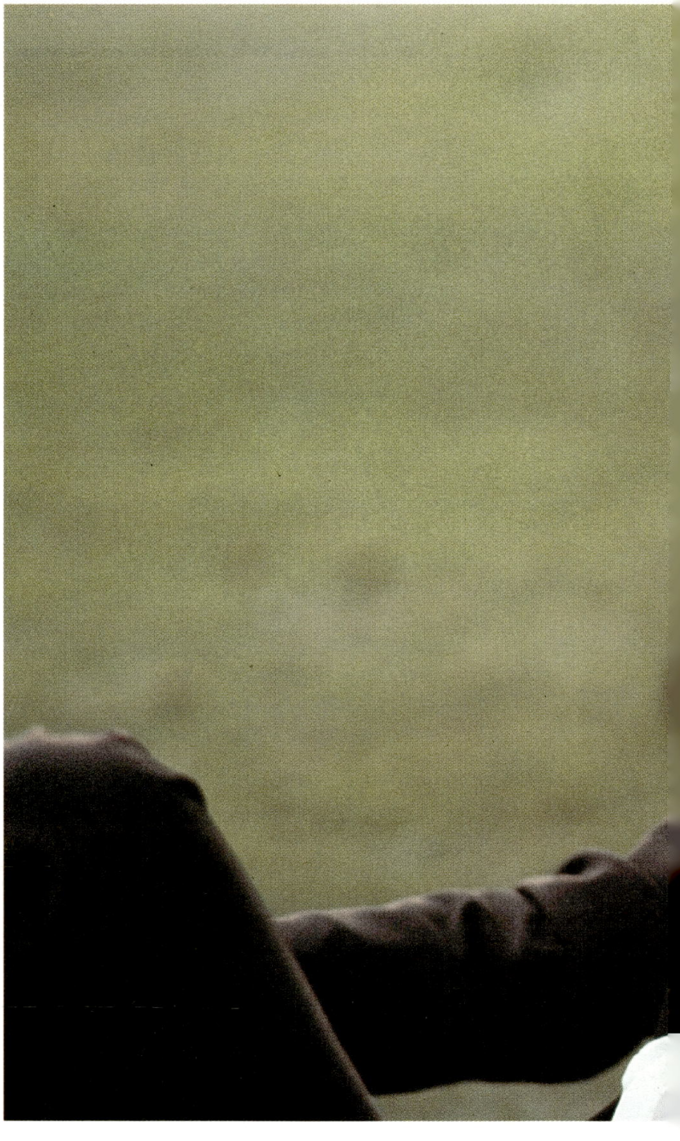

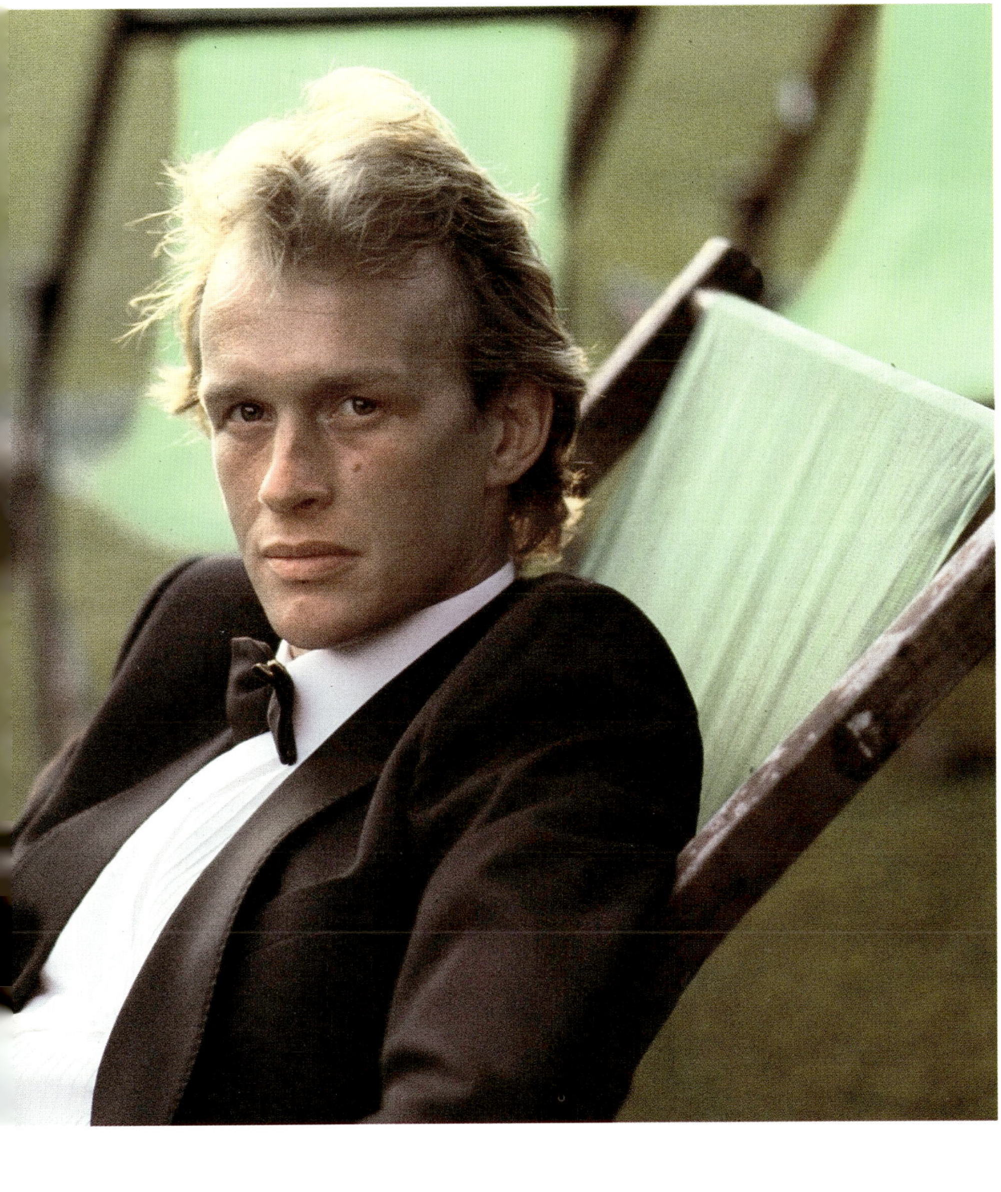

He was so mean and moody
Up-front, nothing to hide
This young man and his shining Porsche
Could soon take me for a ride

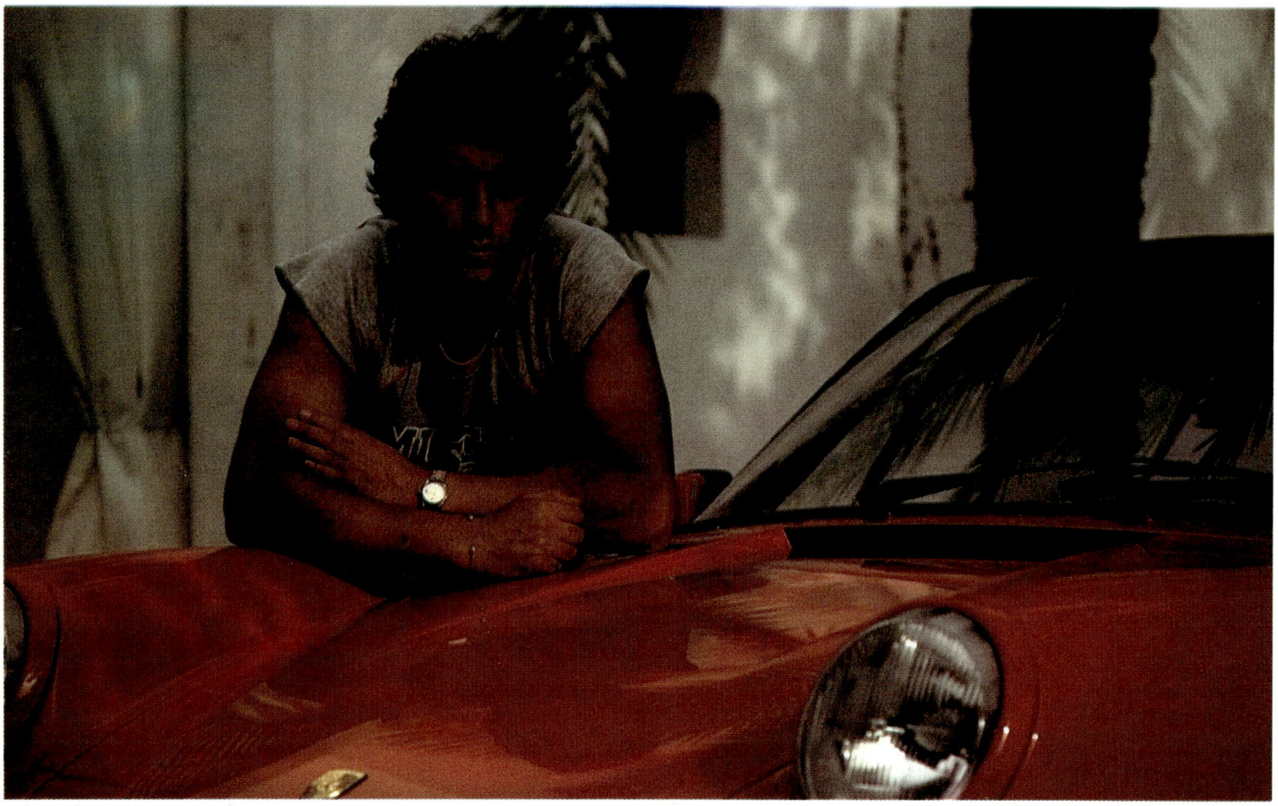

The chappie on the yellow chair
Isn't wearing any clothes
The only thing he's covered
Seems to be above his nose

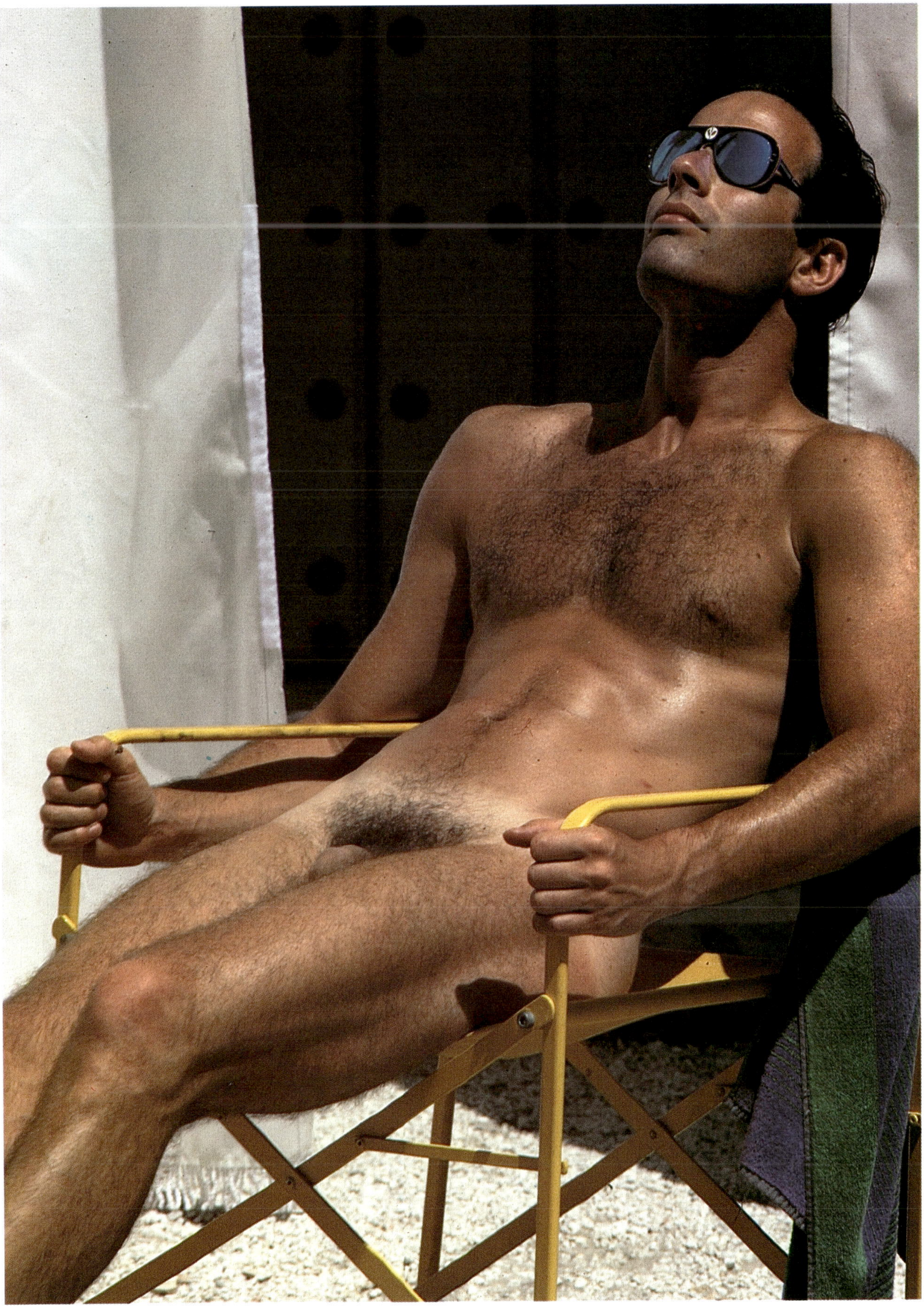

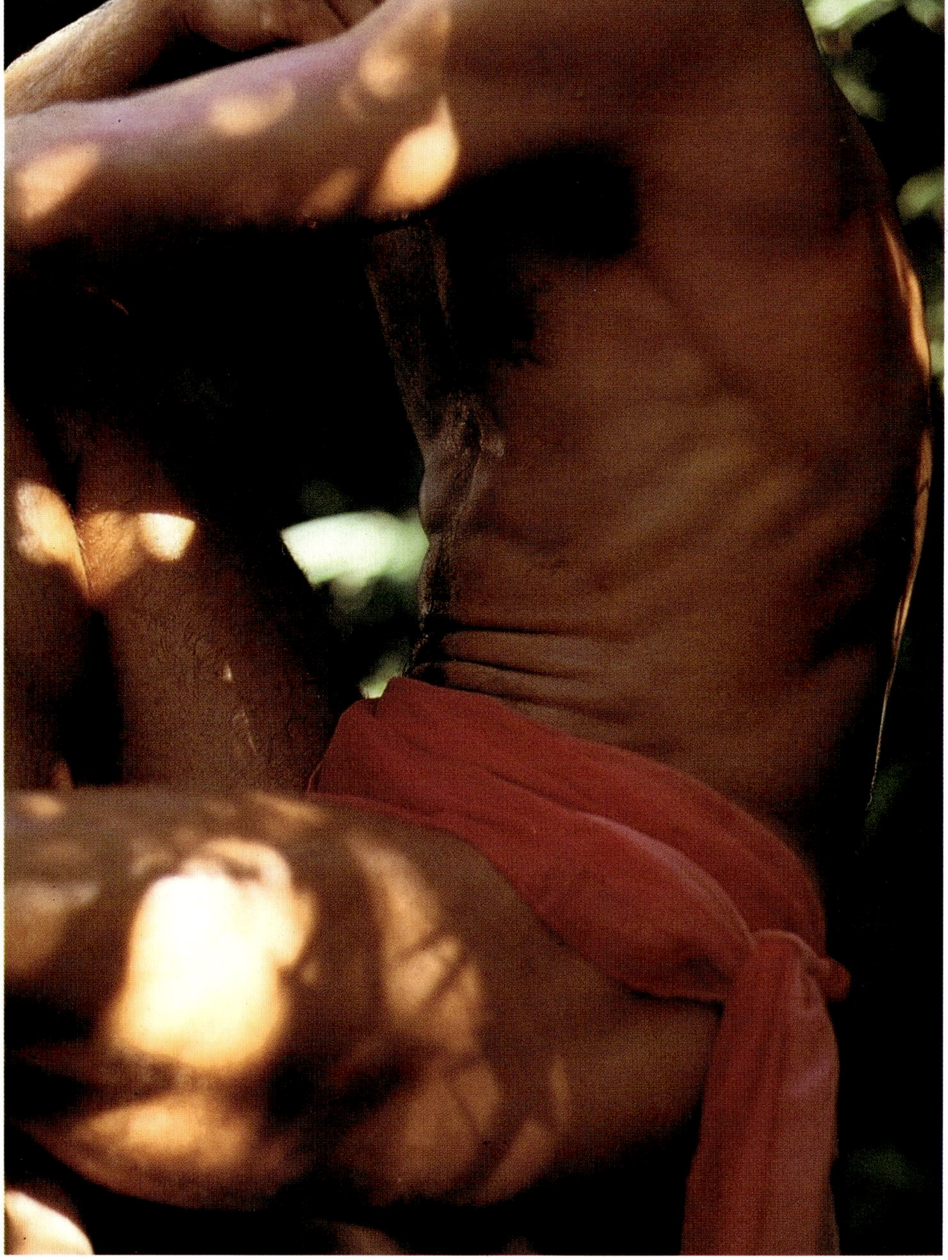

He reminded me of the Greek, Chiron,
Resplendent in his red chiffon
But unlike the torso of that old centaur
I'll remember him for ever more

This really is a Dapper Dan
In his case, Dapper Danny
He looks a suave and dangerous man
Just tailor-made for me
Oh, Danny Boy, you look so smart
You're the one that stole my heart

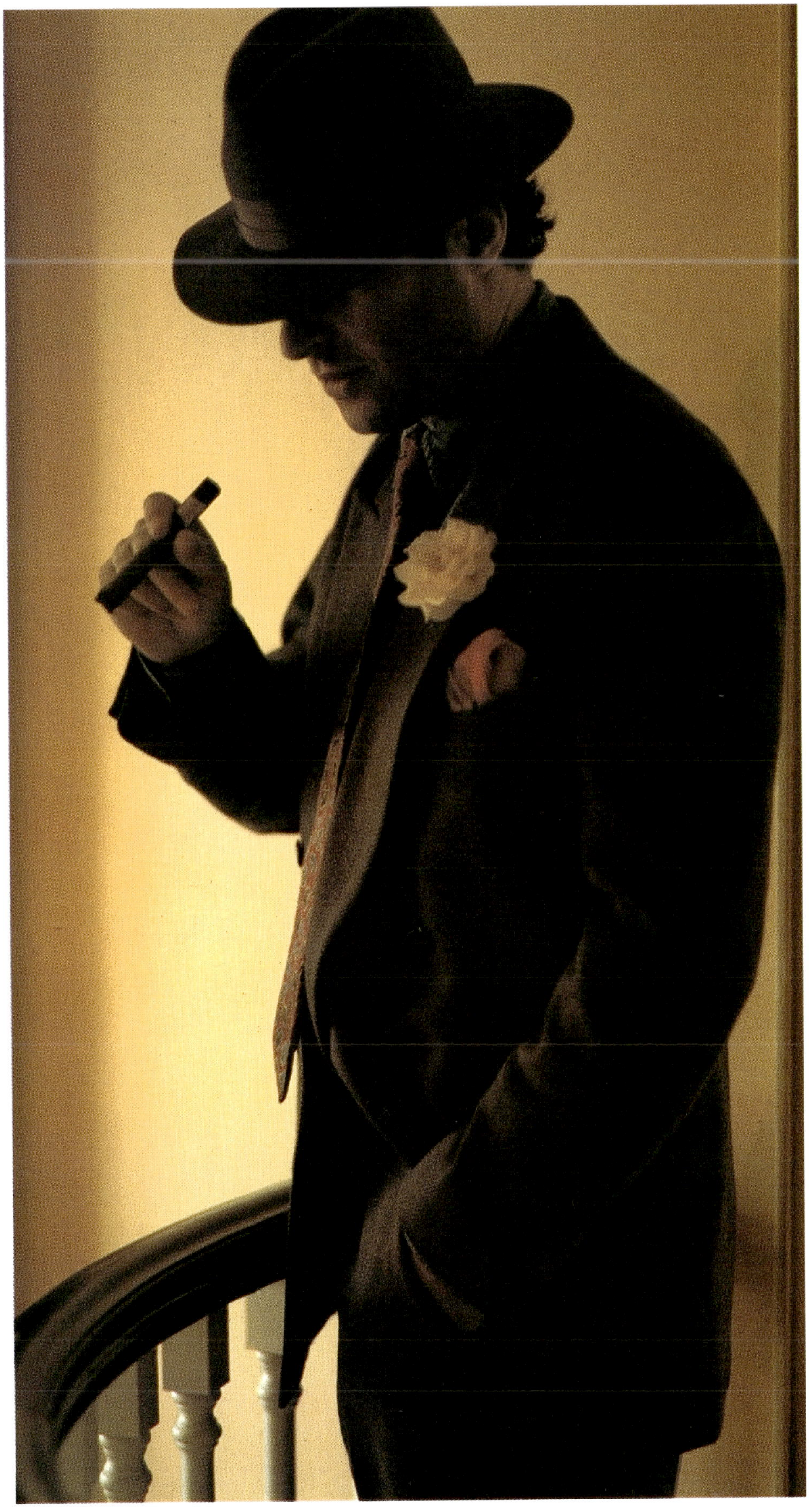

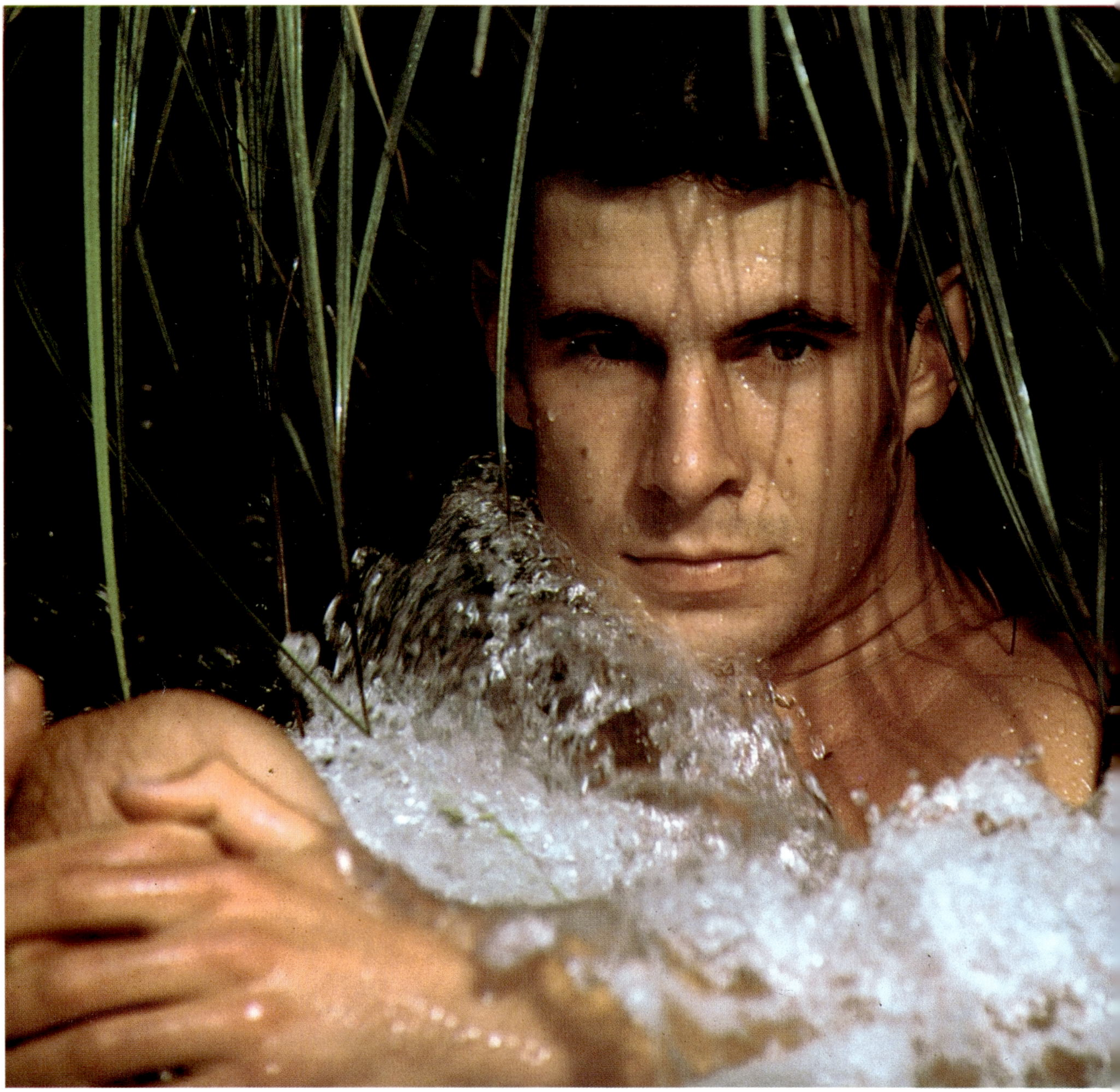

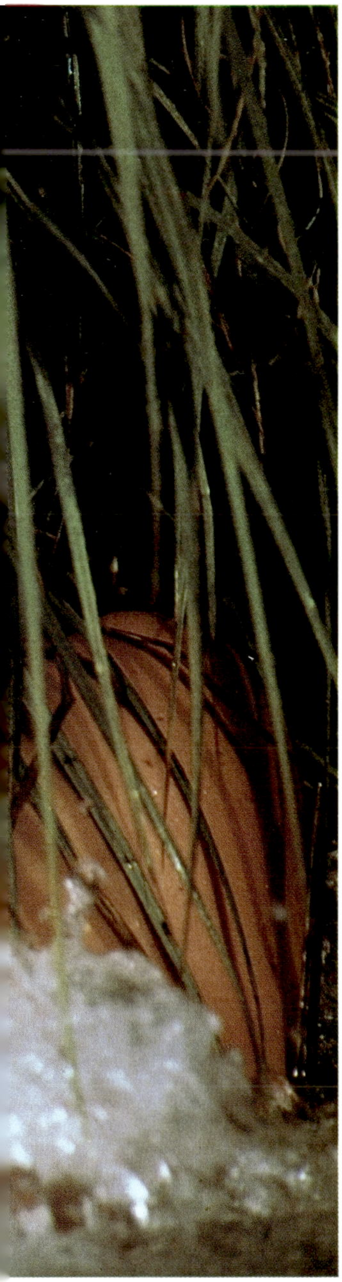

The man looking up from the river's edge
Made me stop and think
He's going to a lot of trouble
Just to get a drink

I saw them playing in the sun
This young man and his hound
They looked like they were having fun
I didn't make a sound
I thought it might be nice if he
Took me for a walkie

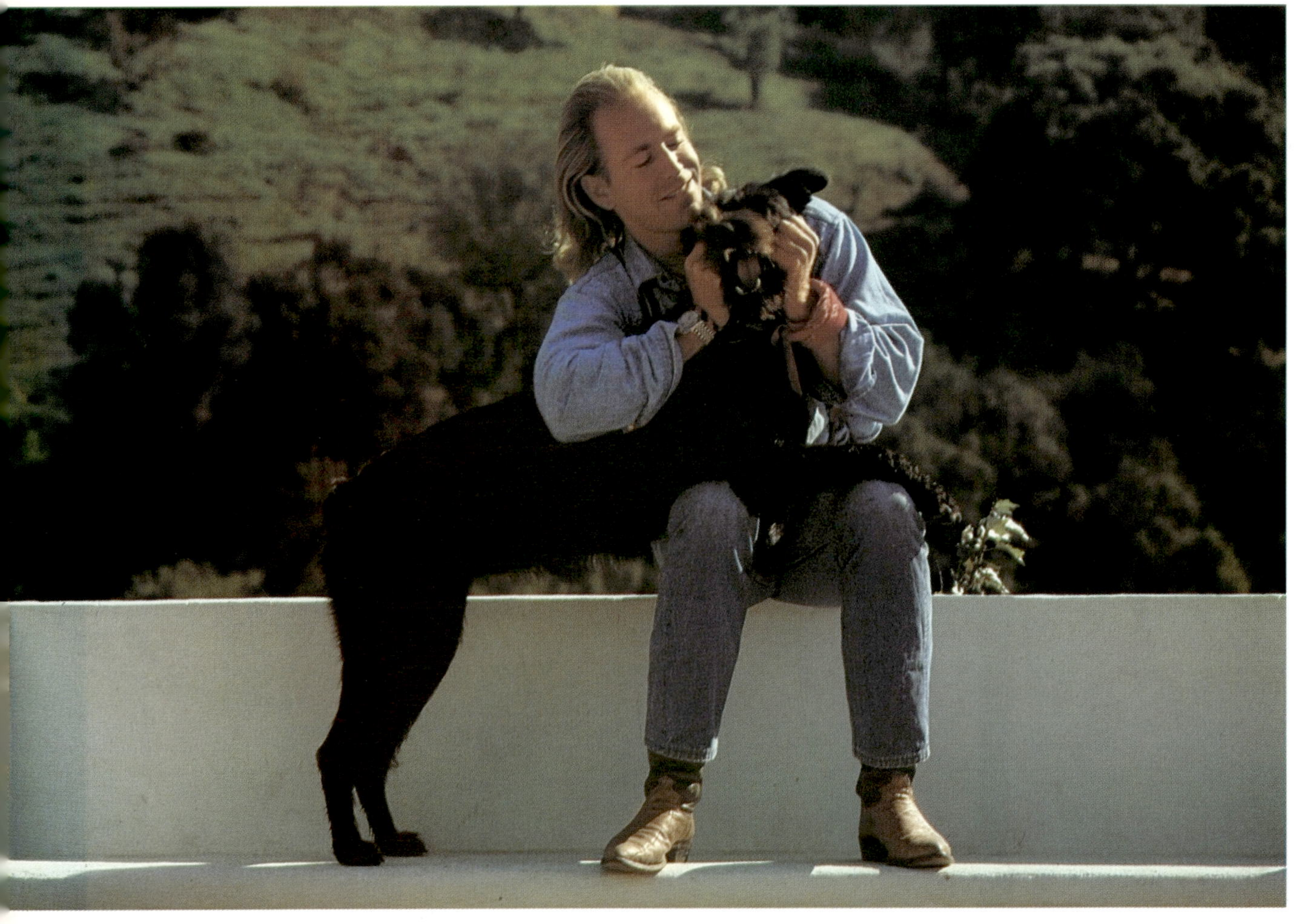

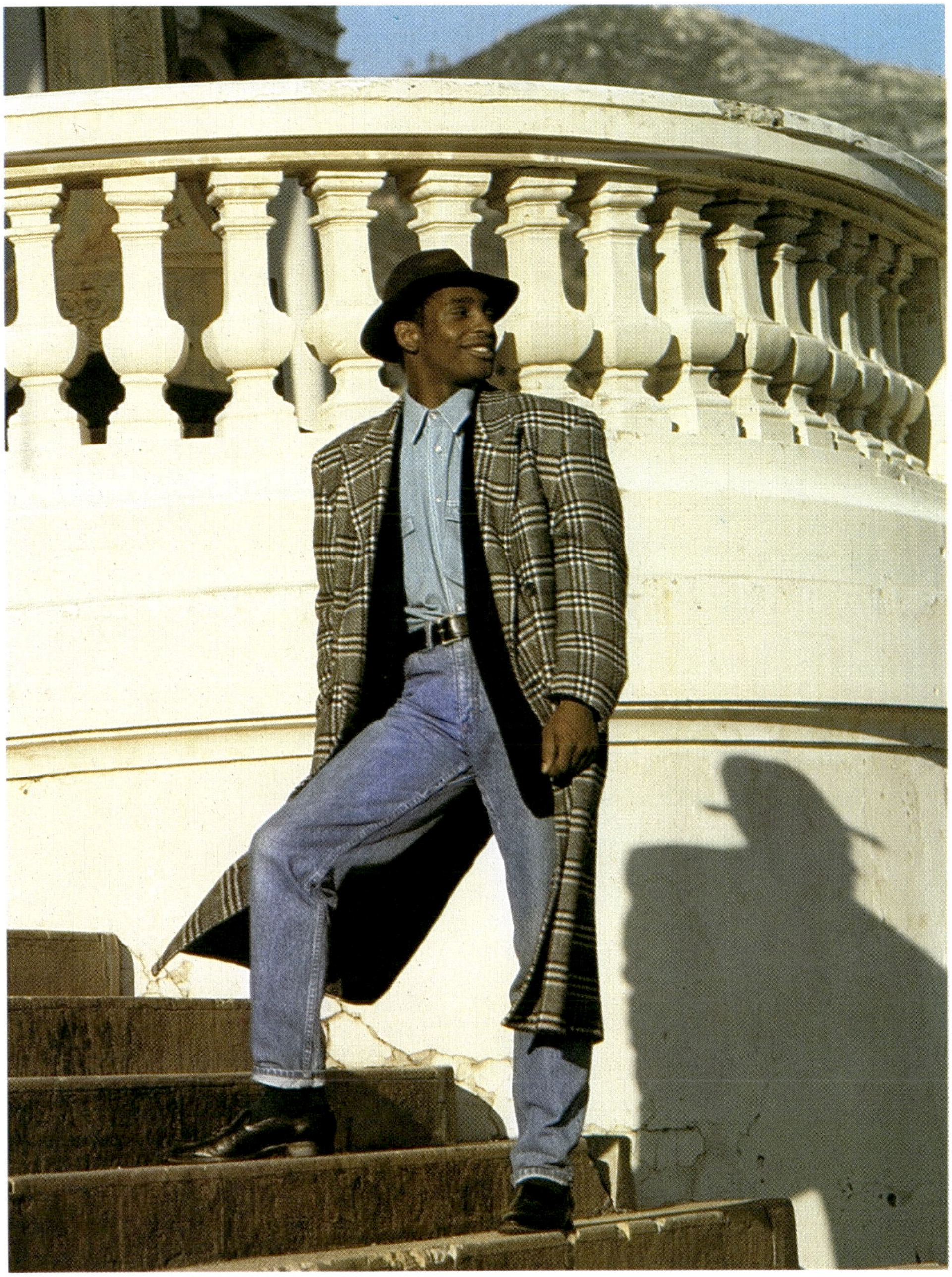

At Monte Carlo on the steps
Climbing up to place his bets
Mr Cool likes lansquenet
And spins a wheel with no regret
Gambling to him is not a threat
But then he hasn't met me yet

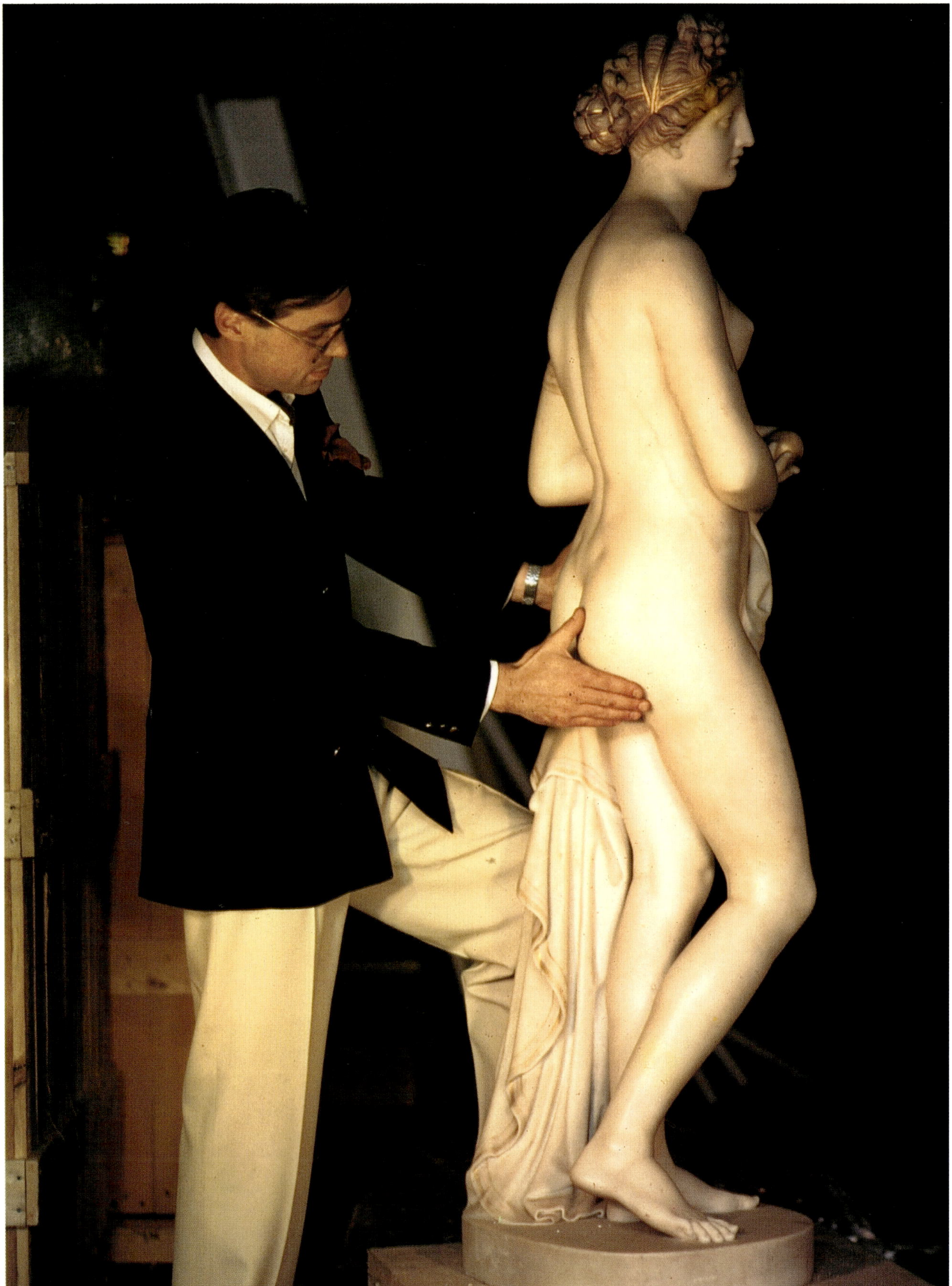

The Prince gazed on the Tinted Venus
Entralled by this work of art
It was the only thing between us
It kept us both apart
The young man was enraptured
That anyone could see
He made me wonder to myself
Could he feel that way for me?

I watched him ride the waves
This young man by the sea
I wondered about his surfboard
Could there be room aboard for me?

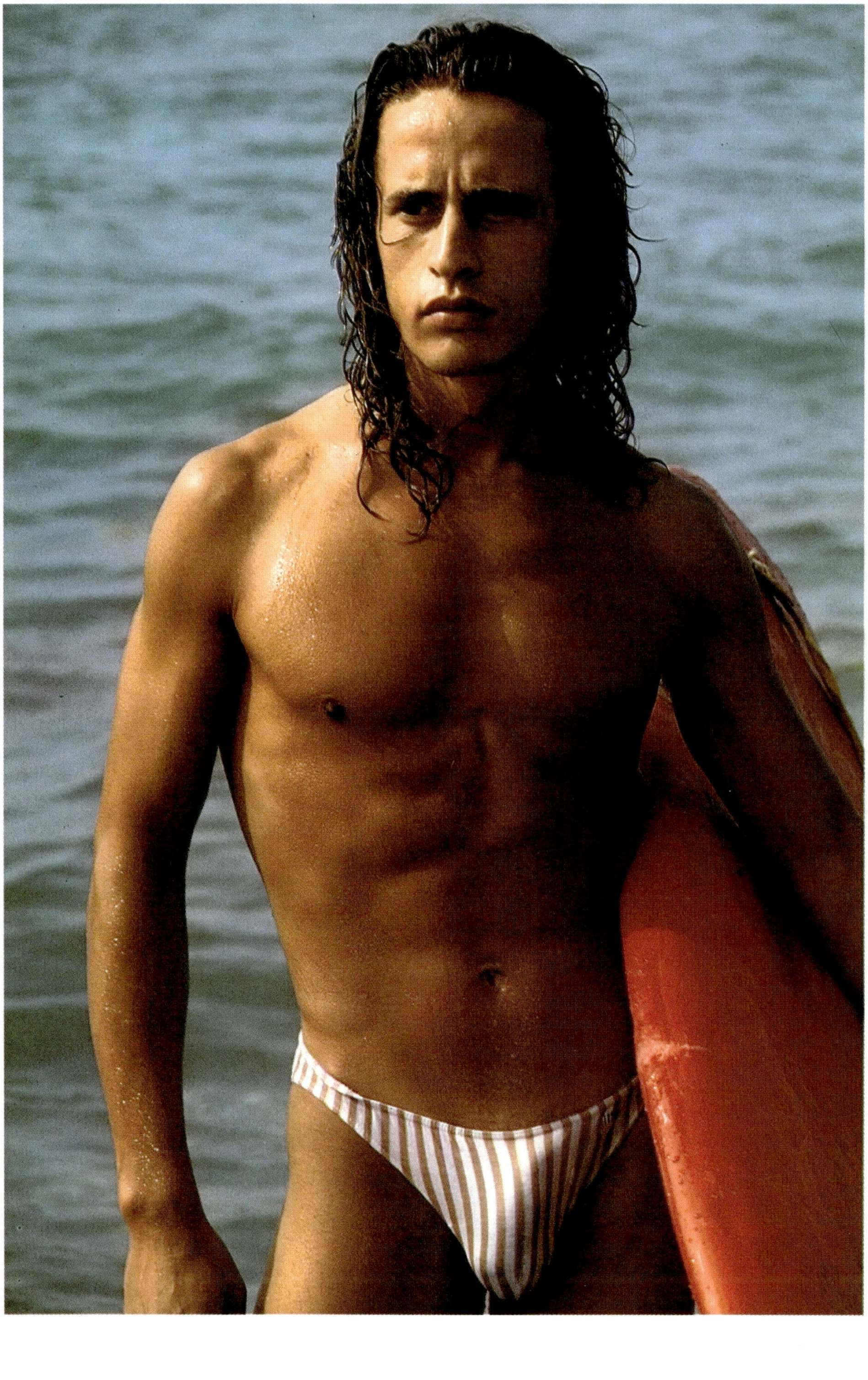

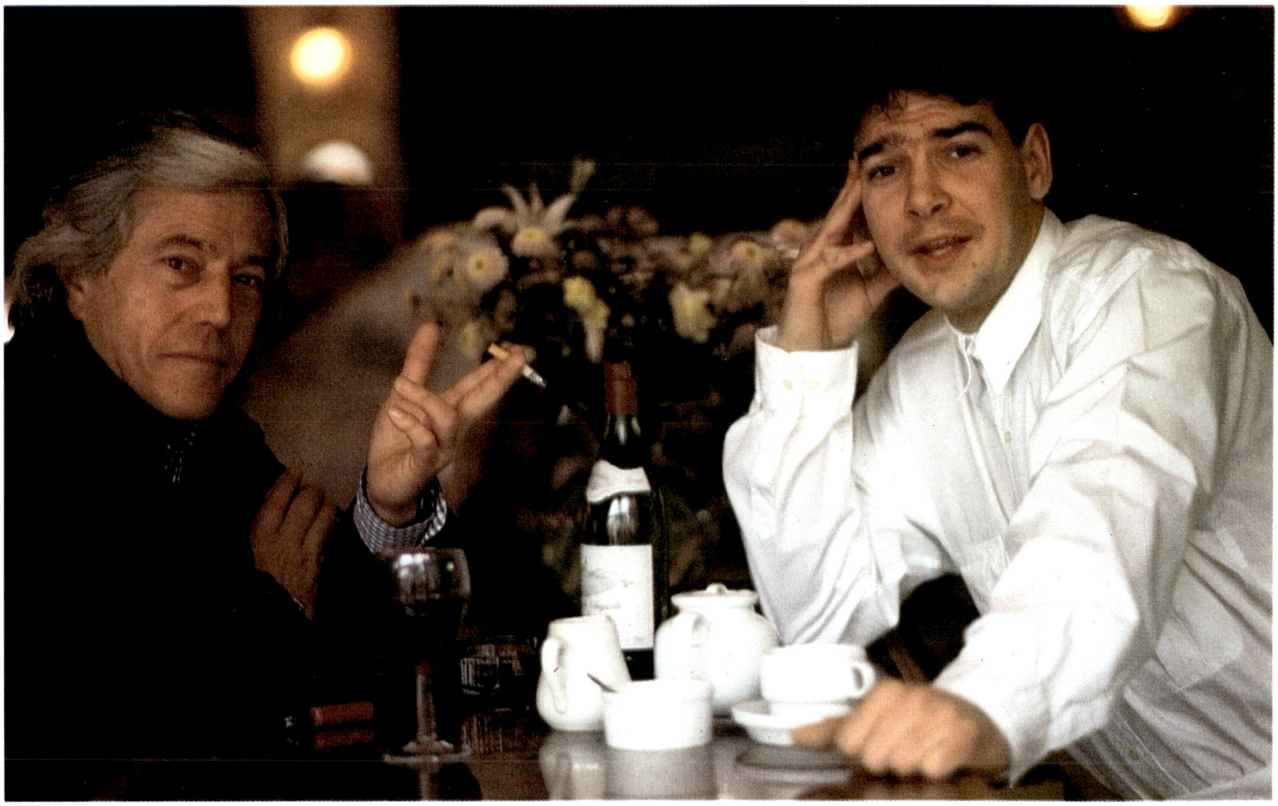

I wonder what they're looking at—
These two chaps having such a chat—
Are they discussing ornithomancy?
Something, it seems, has taken their fancy

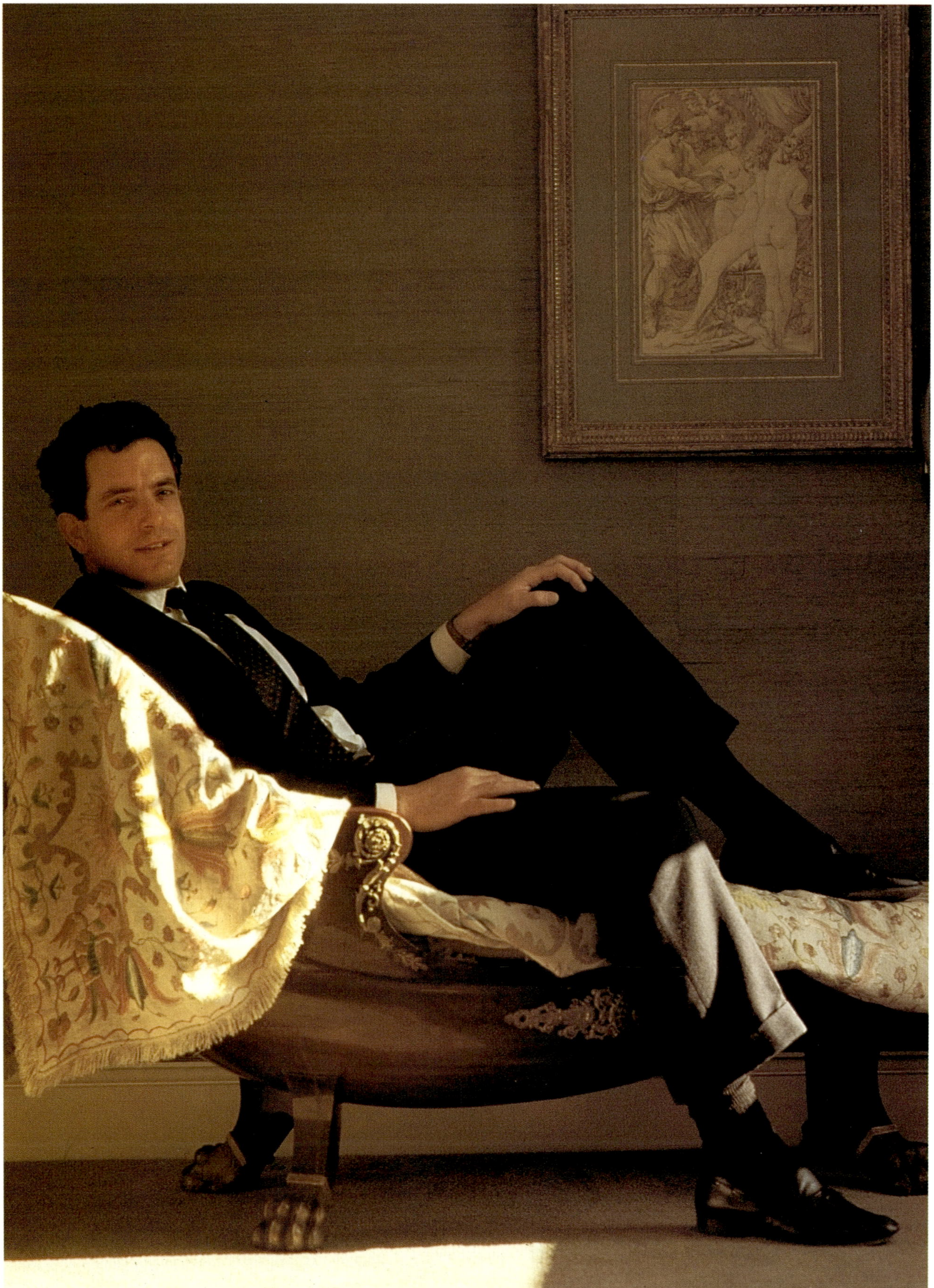

He sat in calm tranquillity
The young man on the sofa
Was he deep in meditation
Or just an idle loafer?

Before a portrait of a Russian dancer –
Nijinsky, that well-known prancer –
Danced a youth so picturesque
His arabesque was statuesque
Would I join him in a pas de deux?
Yes, sir

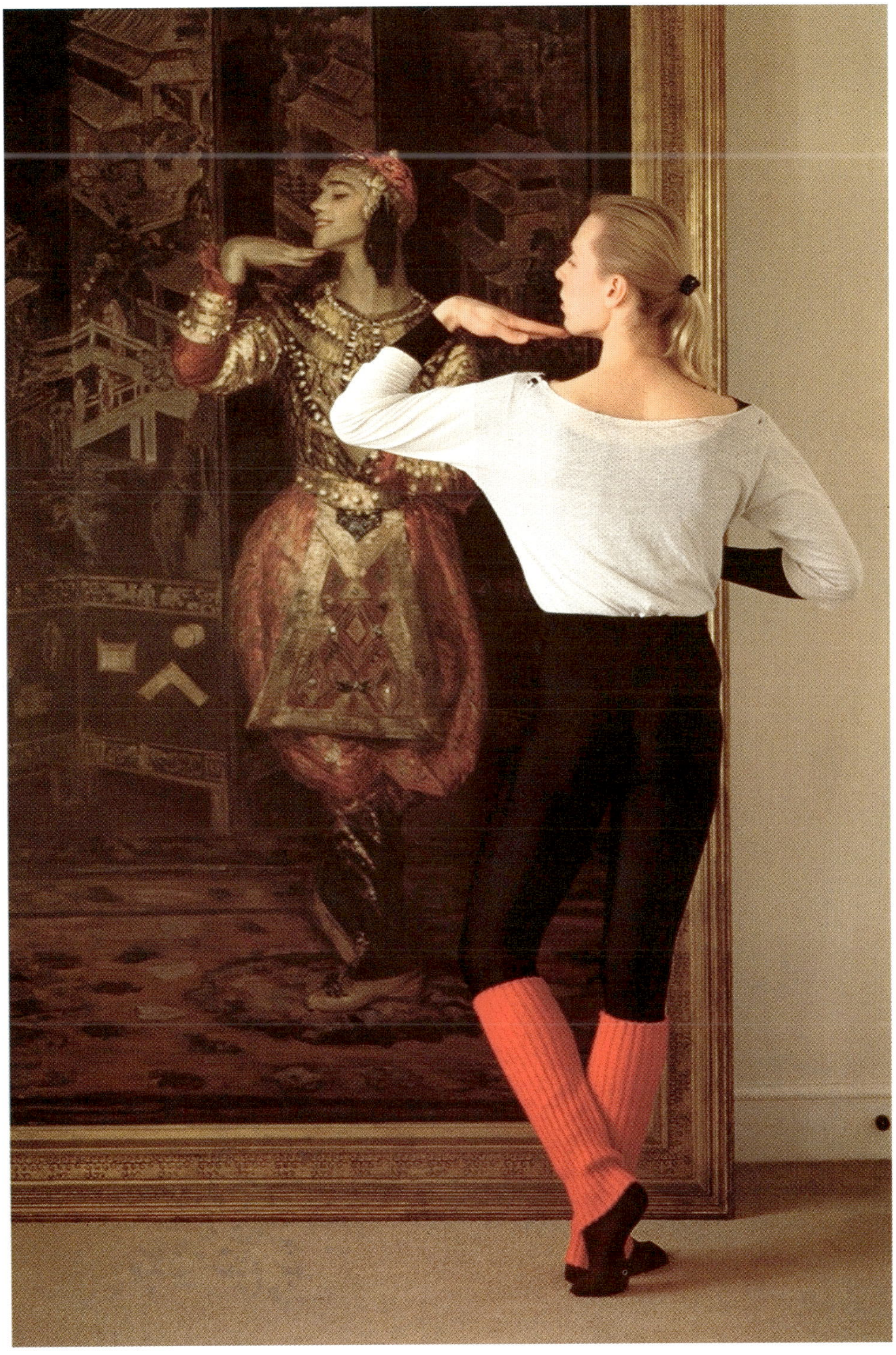

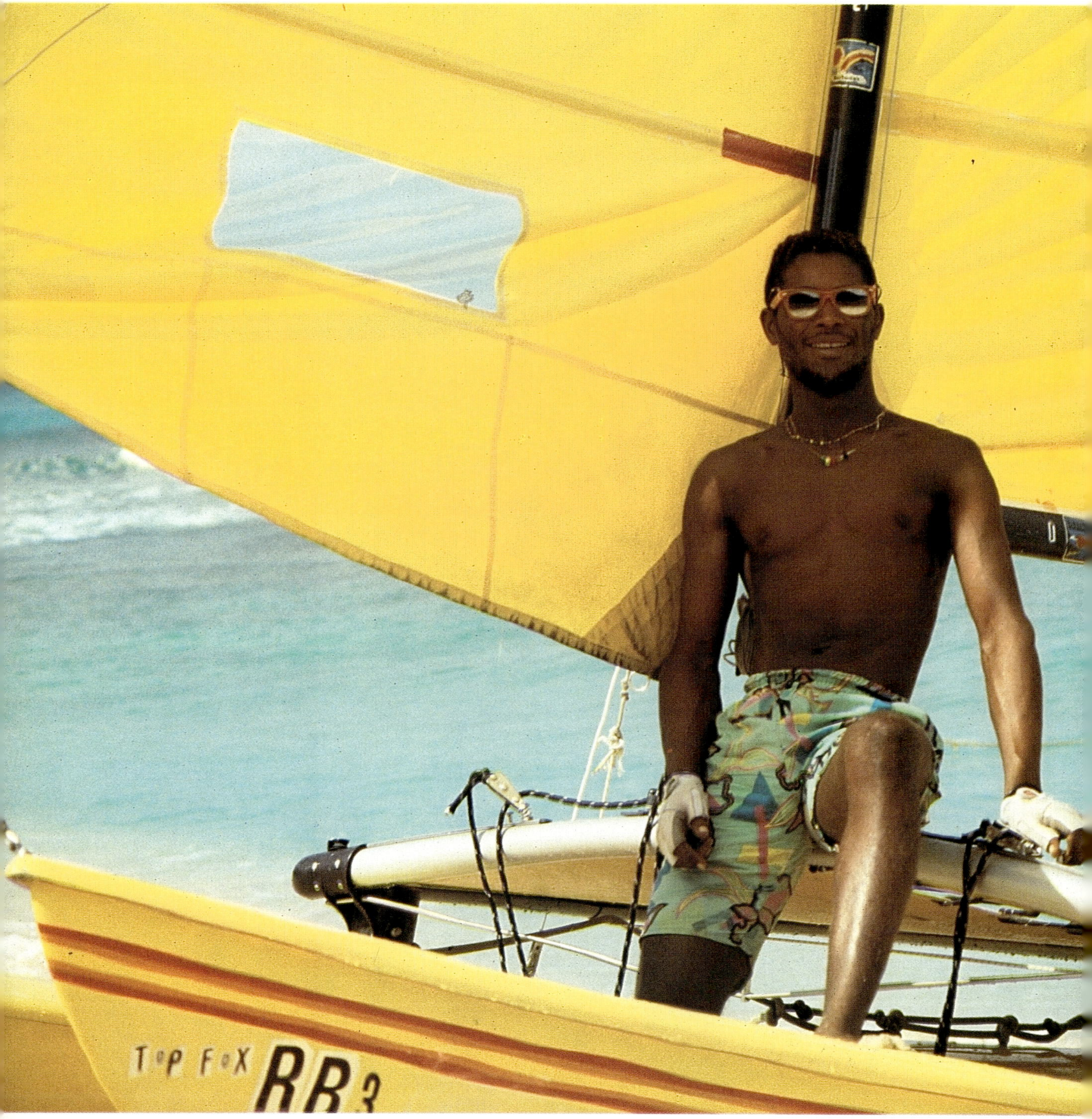

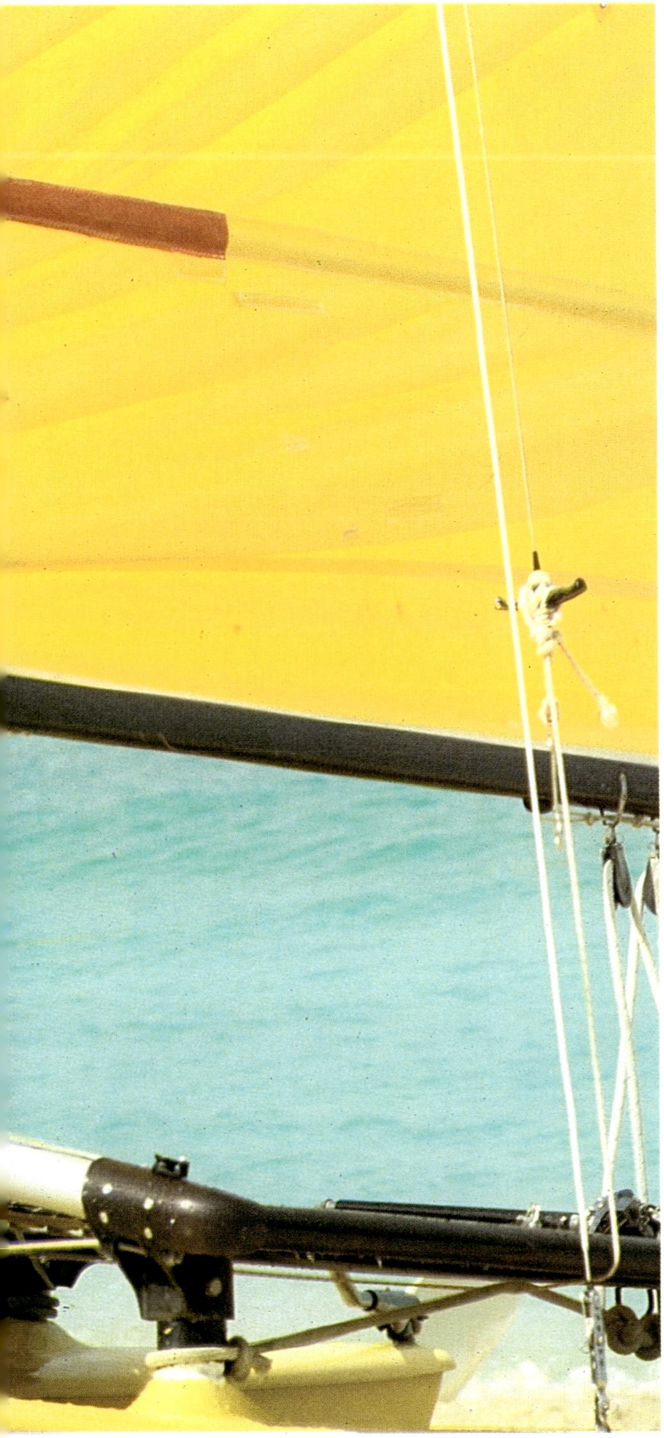

The boy sat on the burning deck
Although there weren't any flames
The heat came from the noonday sun
I'll bet there'll be games when it wanes

I can certainly see the attraction—
A girl and a shiny sports car
If the boy can talk himself aboard
The journey may not be that far

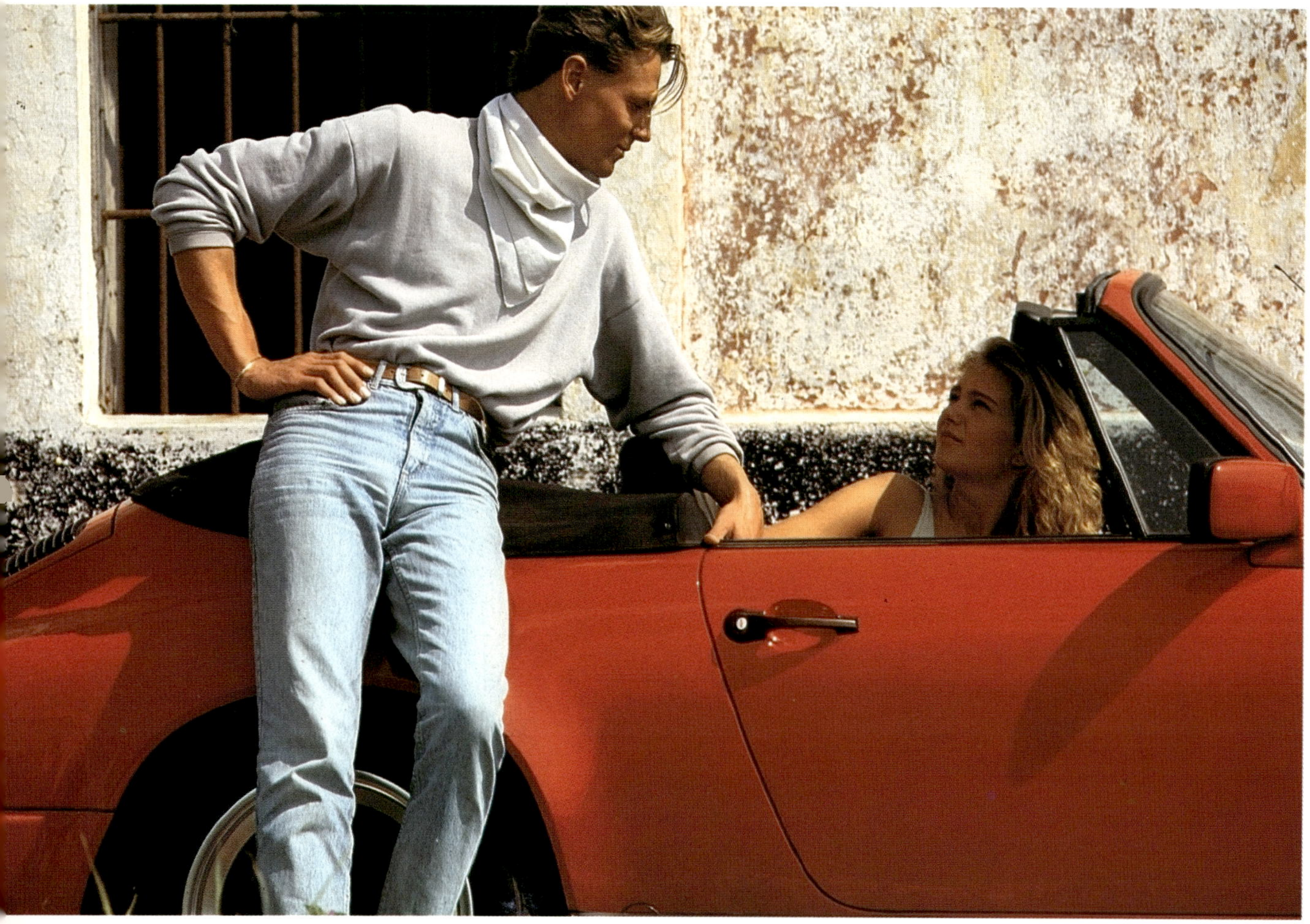

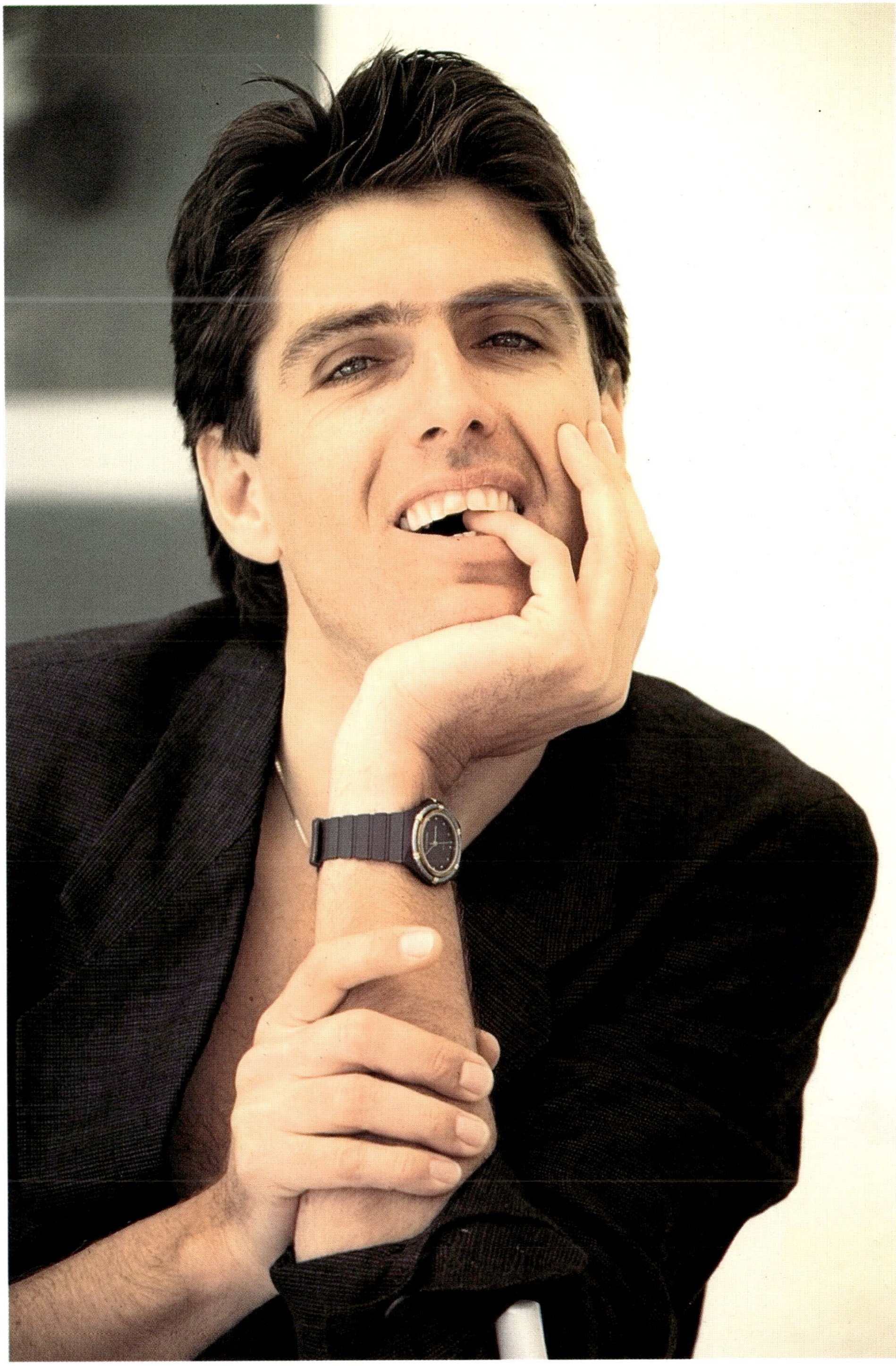

This boy has a deep and
thoughtful look
What does he have in mind?
Is he contemplating life
... or something more refined?

Drinking his coffee all alone
Having a quiet smoke
He seemed to have something on his mind
A moody sort of bloke
But then he smiled and waved to me
Would I join him for a Coke?
A drink would be fine with me—
Champagne though, Coke's a joke

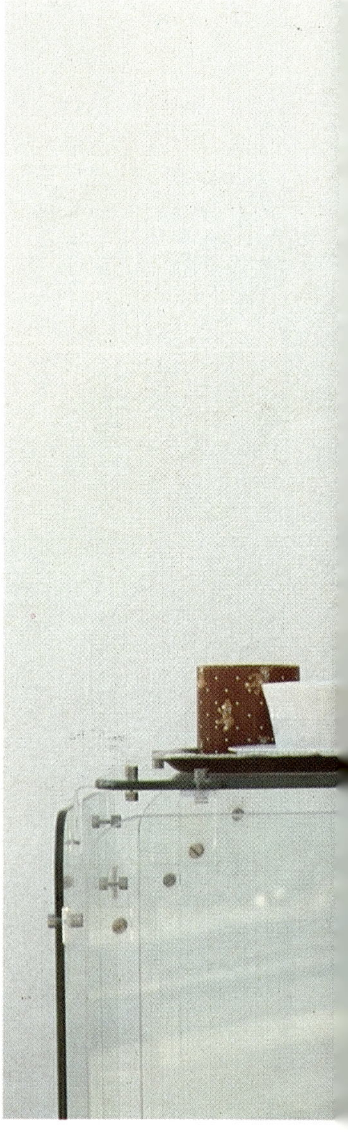

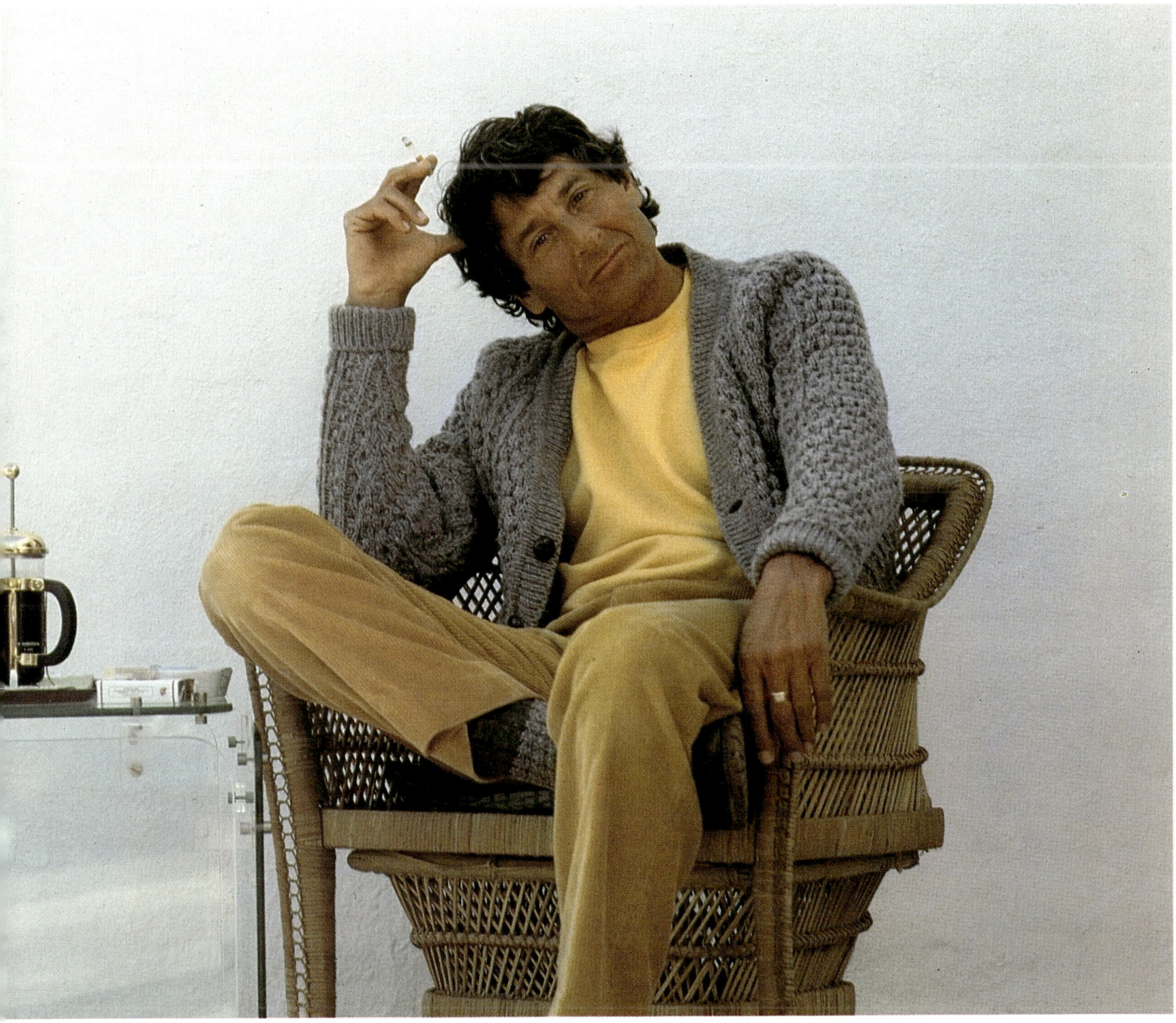

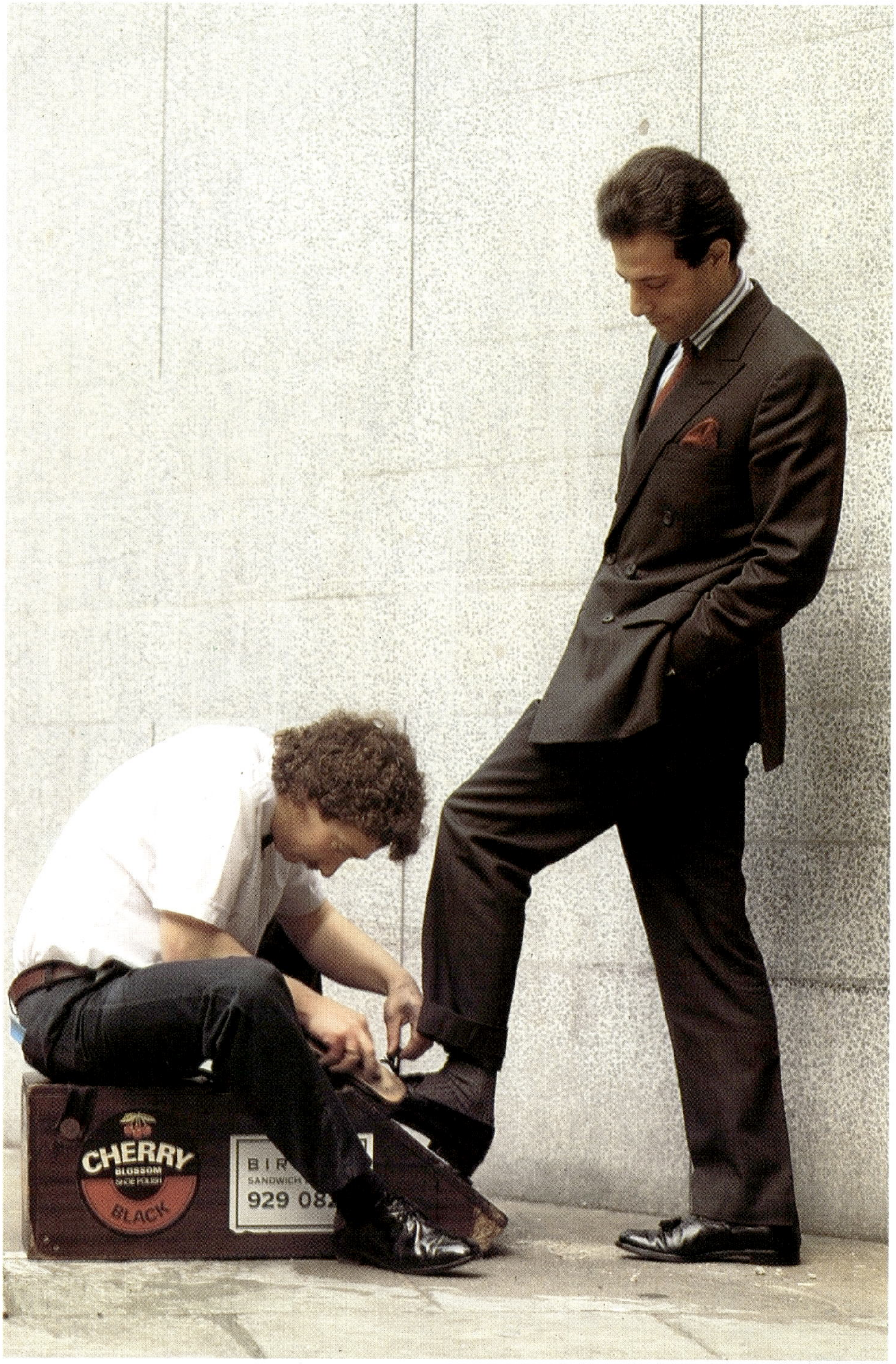

Here is one of our smart young dudes
An air of elegance he exudes
He certainly looks a fine young beau—
His suit was made in Savile Row
His shirt was made in Jermyn Street
St James is where he takes his feet

Then for that final flourish
He gets a shine and polish
And as the young man cleans his shoes
You'll hear him whistle the St Louis Blues

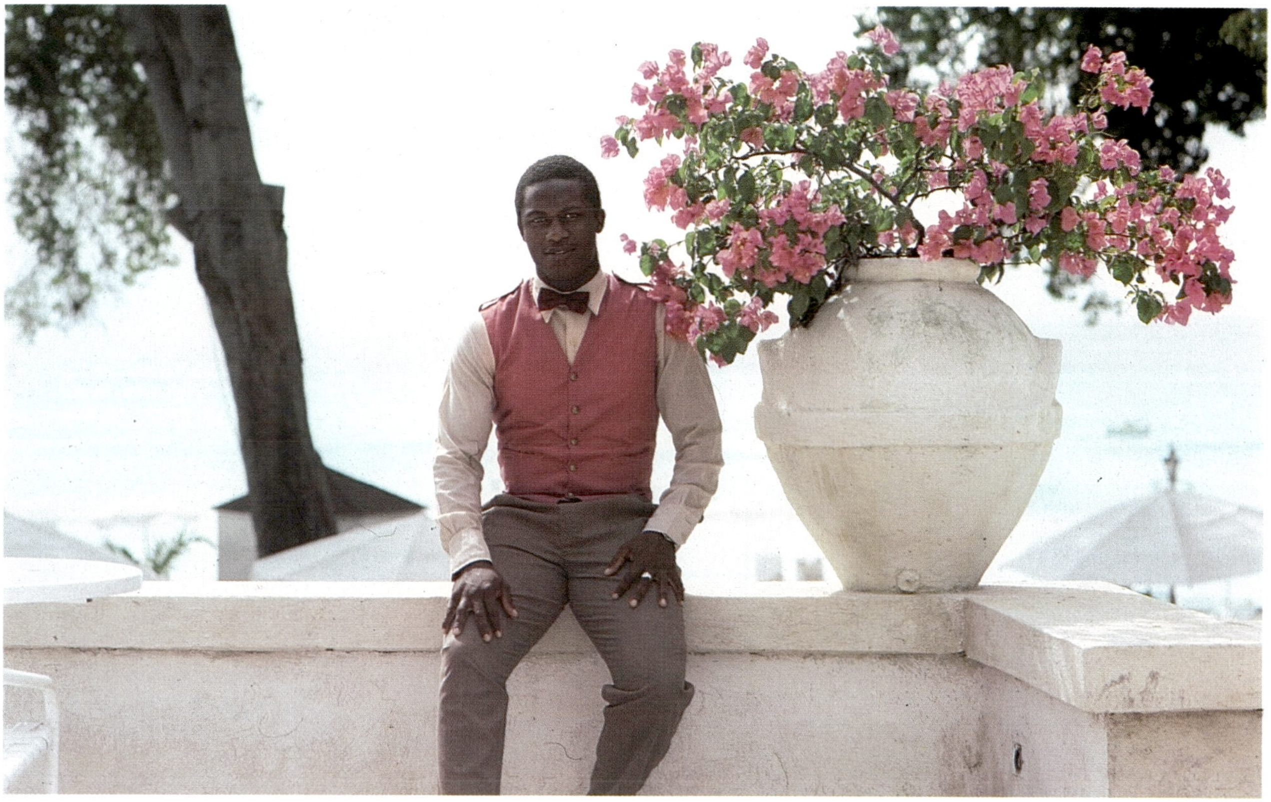

His pink waistcoat and flowers
Made me recall
Those wonderful hours
Spent in an amplexicaul

He rode through the field of wild flowers
Like an ancient cuirassier
This noble dashing horseman
A romantic cavalier

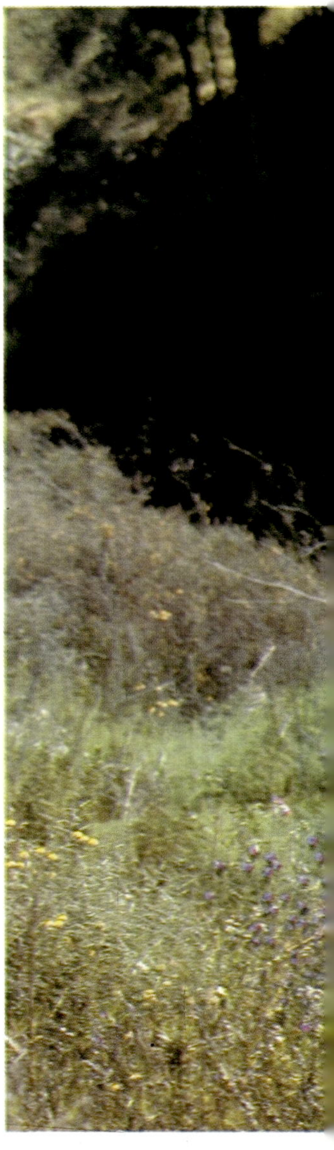

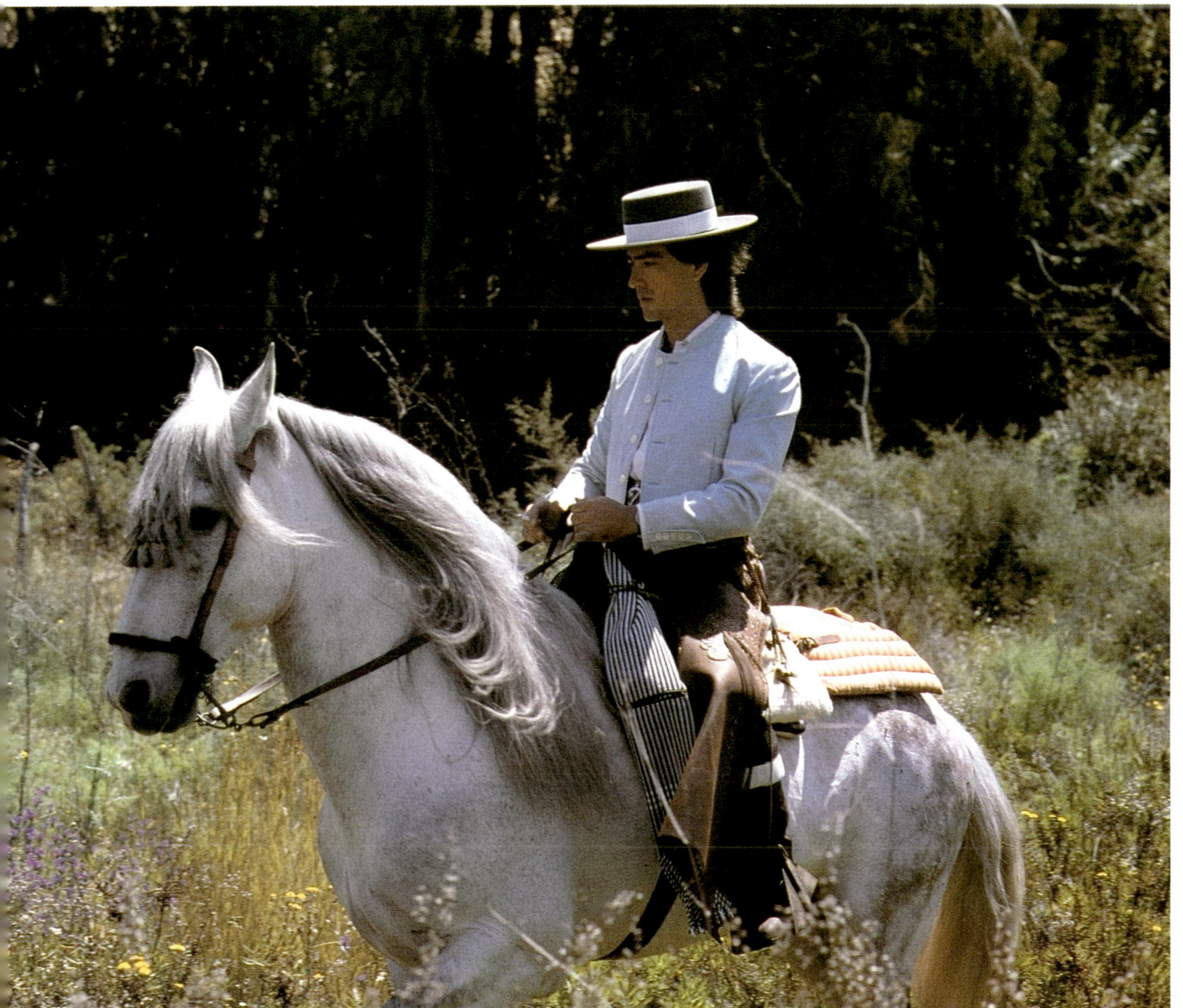

Up aloft the coachman sat
Looking nifty in his saucy hat
But what on earth is on his head
Peeking out beneath his bonnet?
Is it a flamboyant scarf?
Perhaps he wears it for a laugh

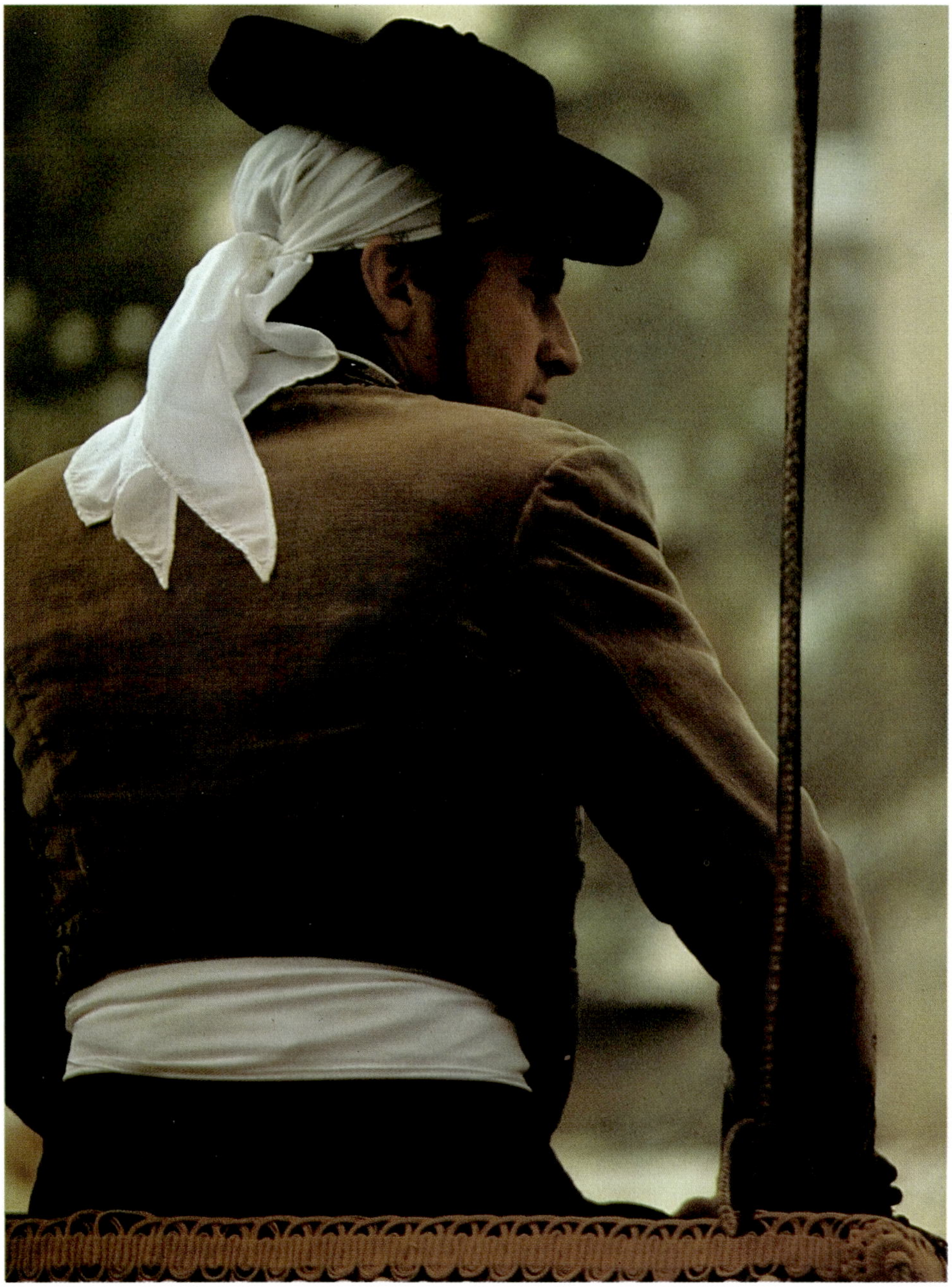

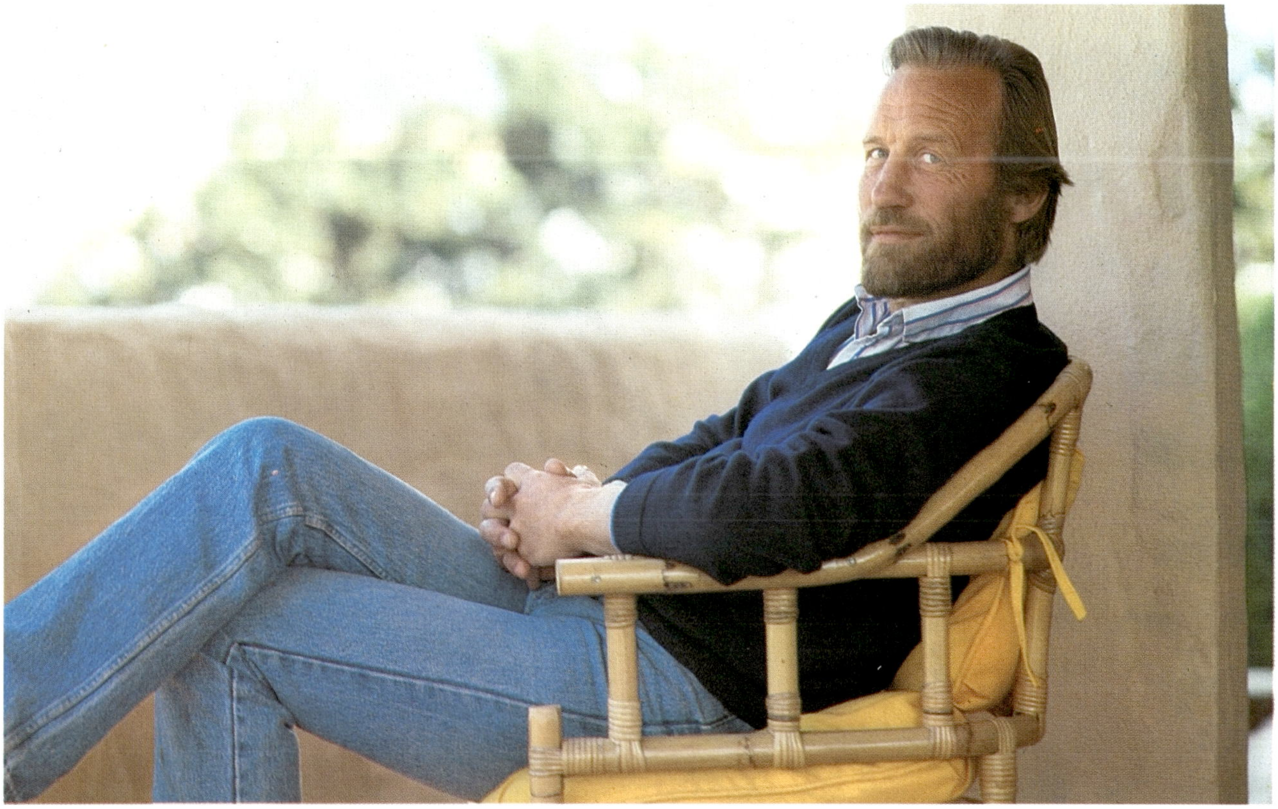

The view from the verandah
To a tall jacaranda
Was a vision of splendour
A joy to the beholder
But watch out, sister
He's not looking at the vista
His eyes aren't gazing at the panorama
He's looking for another type of karma
(Something with a touch of drama?)
This boy's really quite a charmer

The skier looked across at me
Would I join him in a race?
Not now, dear … après *ski*

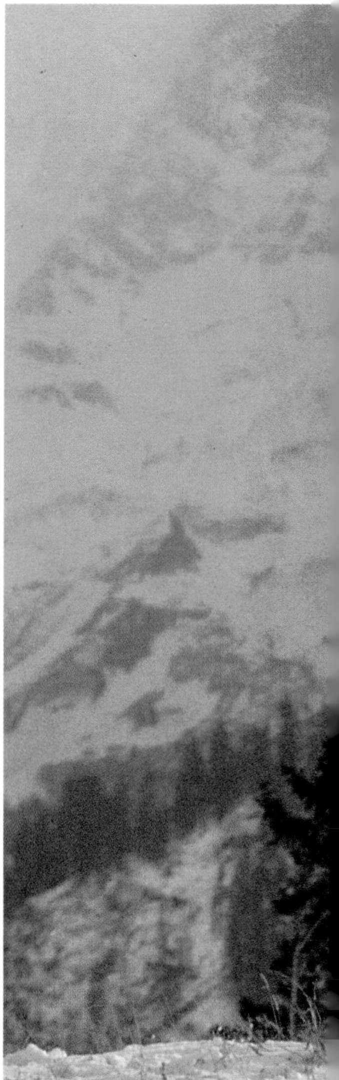

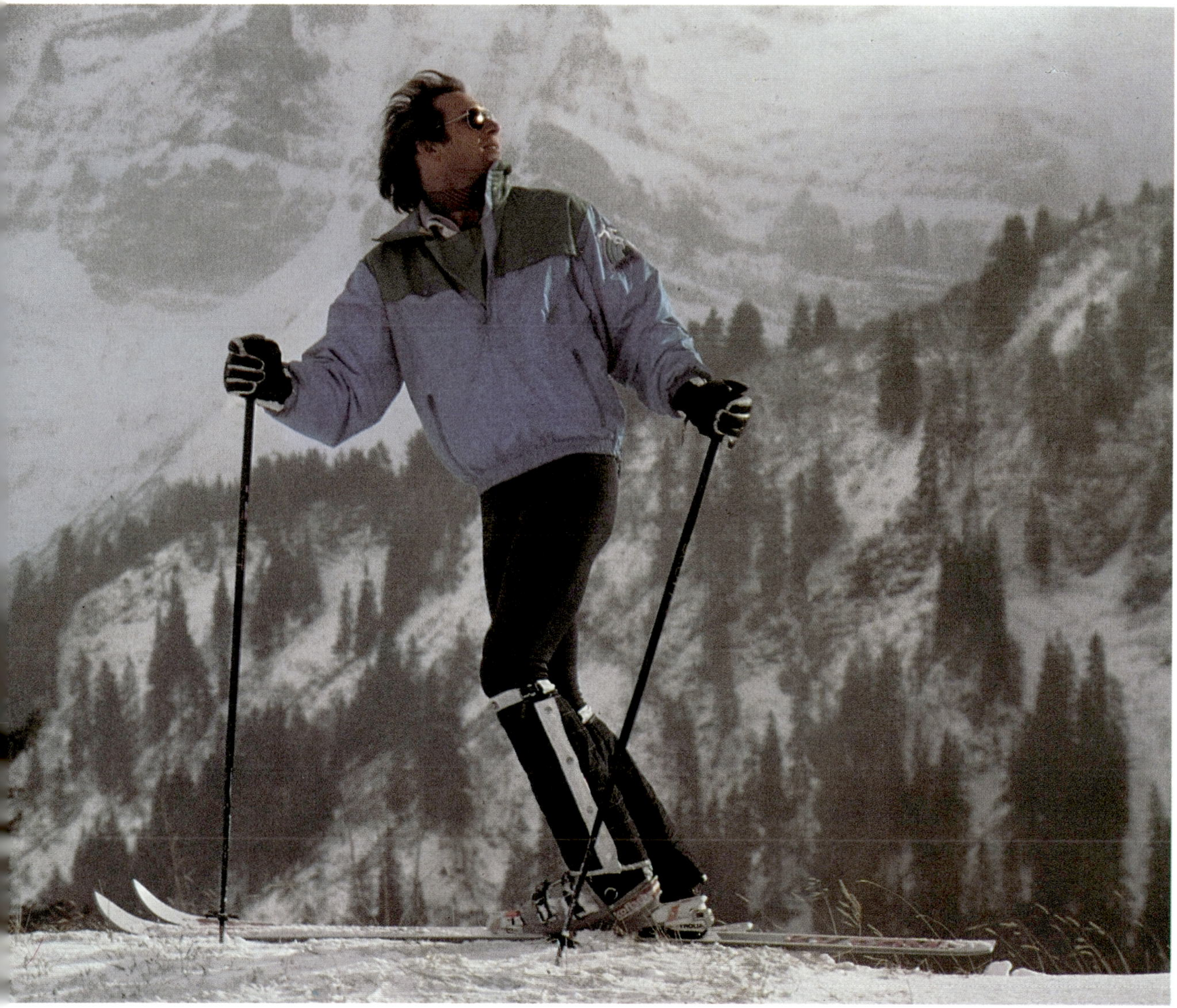

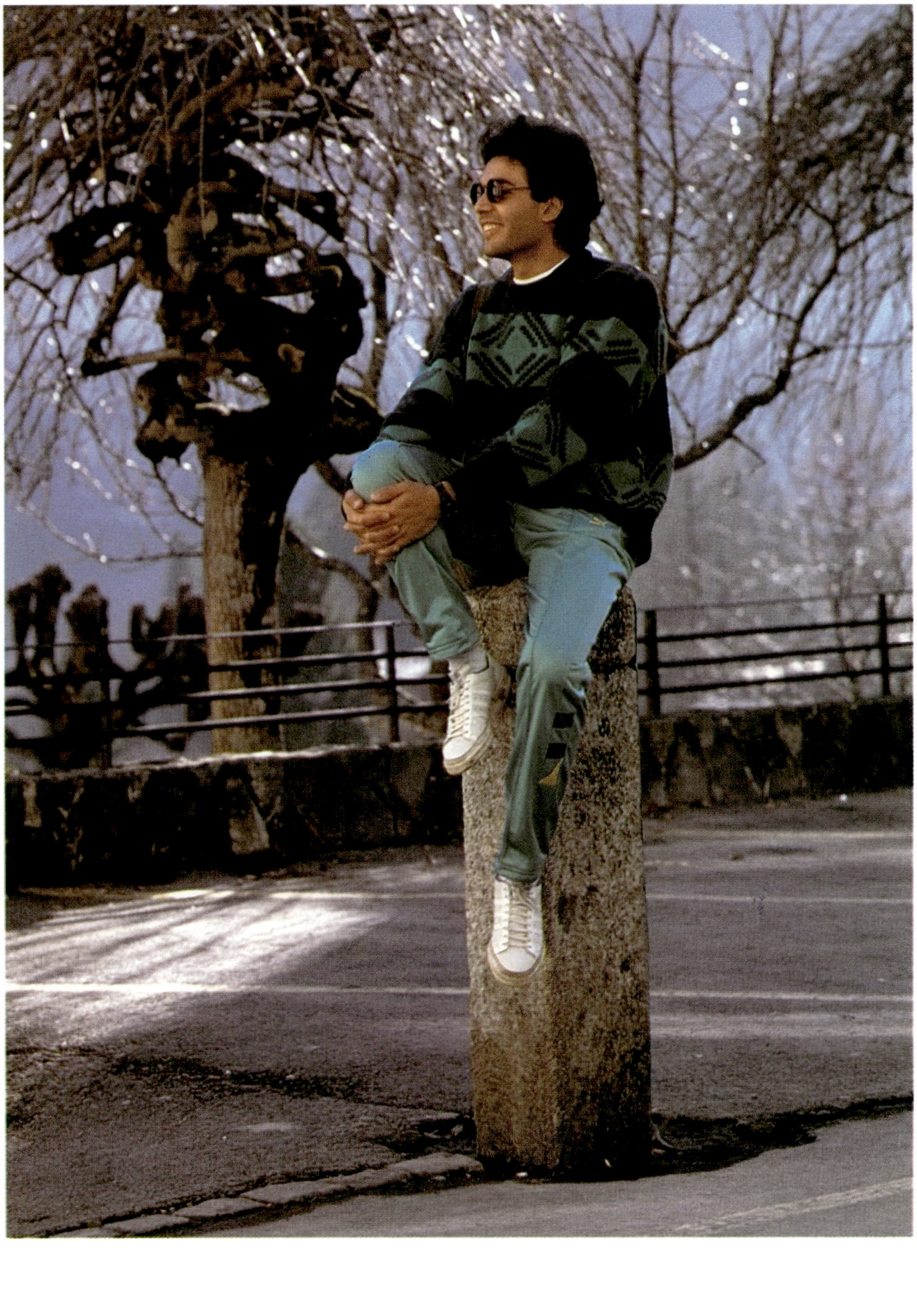

The carefree boy clasped his knee
Sitting by a silver tree
He looked up and smiled my way
Perhaps I'll find a way to stay

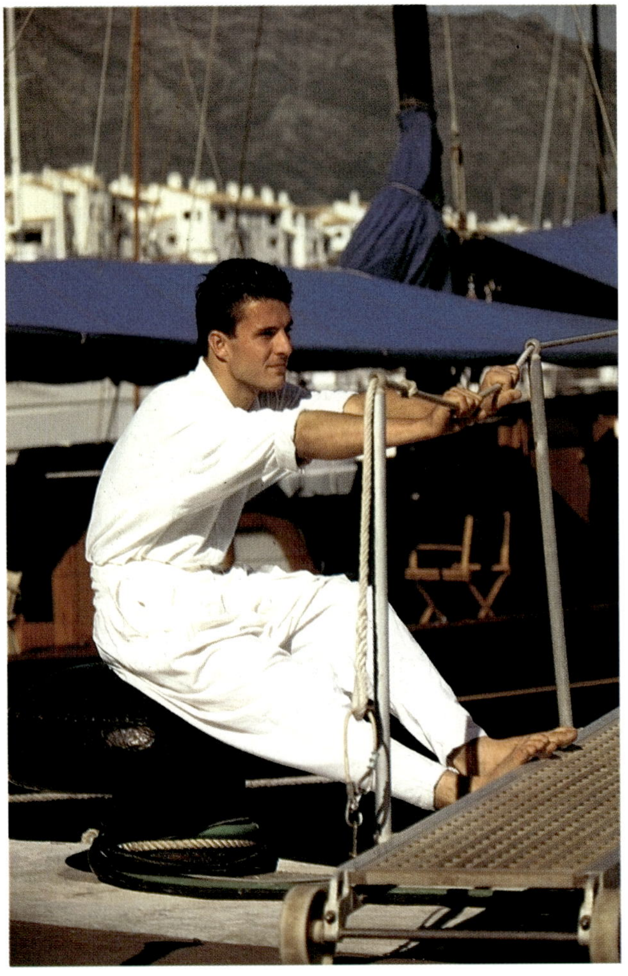

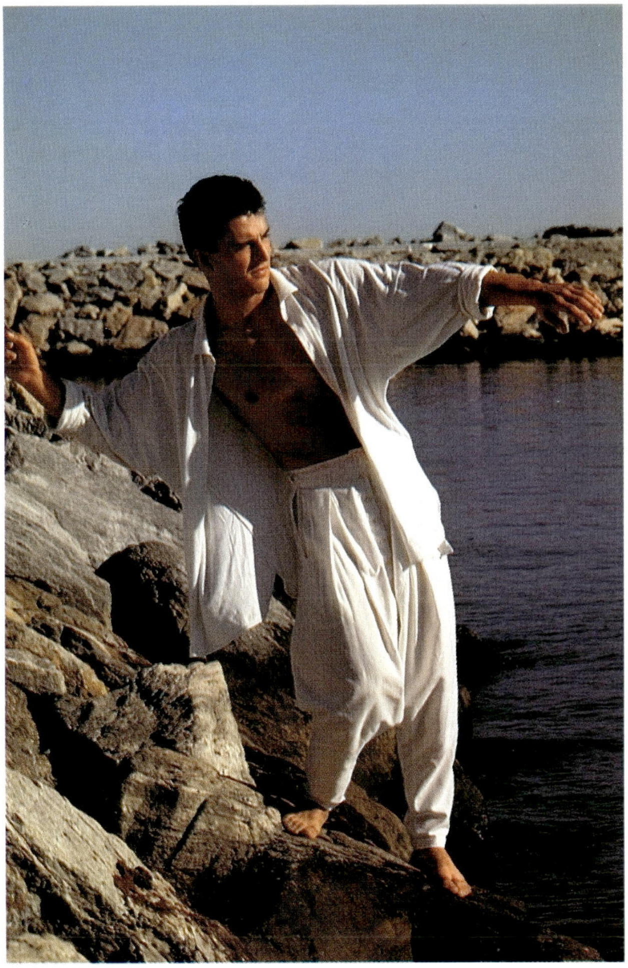

The barefoot boy was throwing rocks
Looking cool without his socks
Those pants of his look very wide
I'm sure there's room for two inside

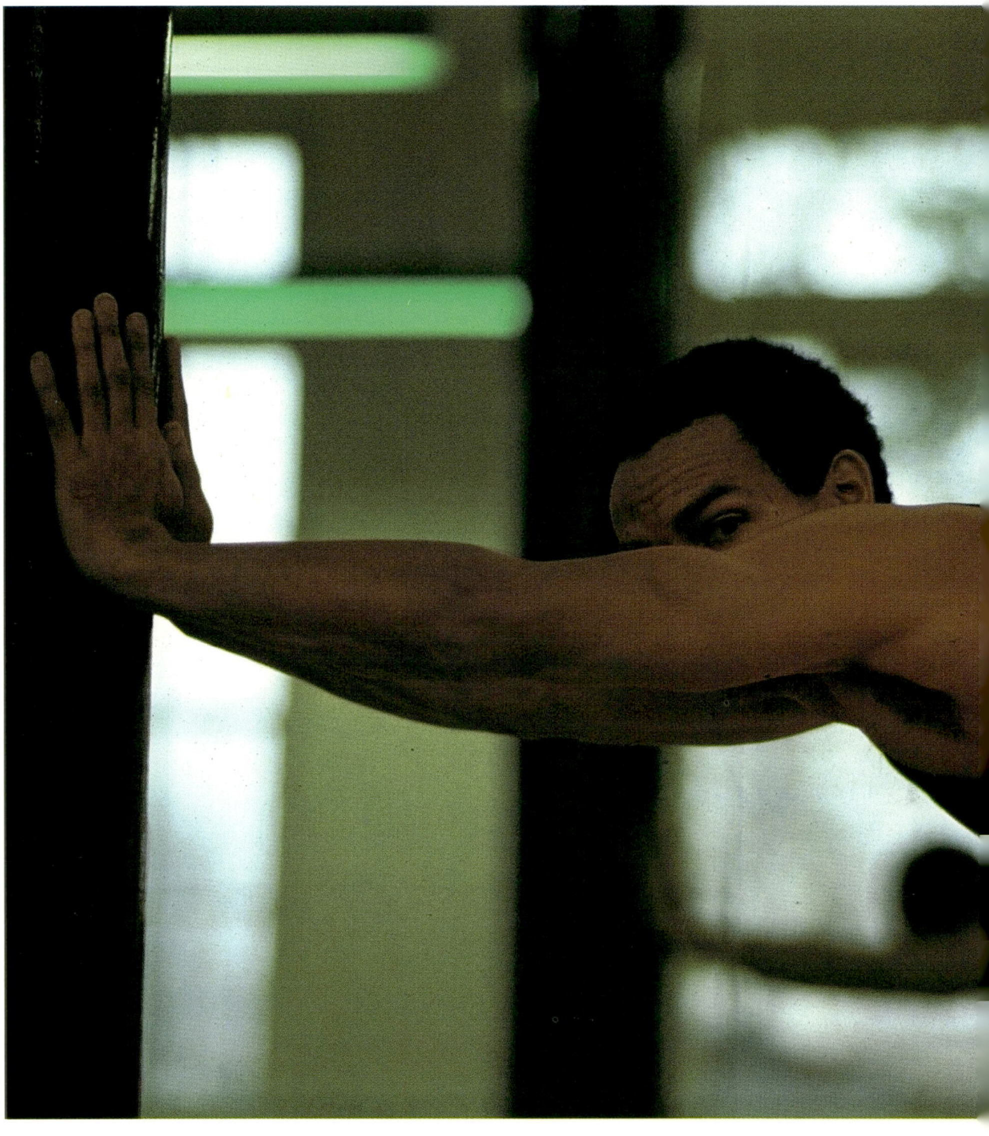

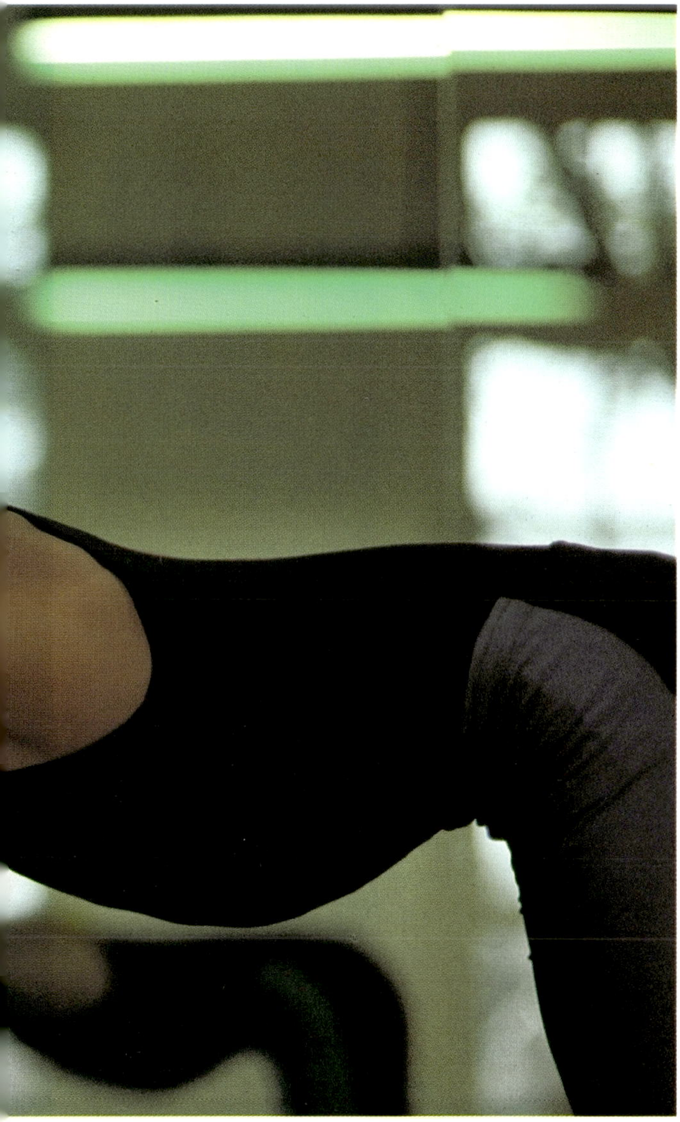

Though in the gym working out
There wasn't any doubt
His mind was on other tussles
Nothing to do with building muscles
And in his eye that wicked look
Captured forever in this book

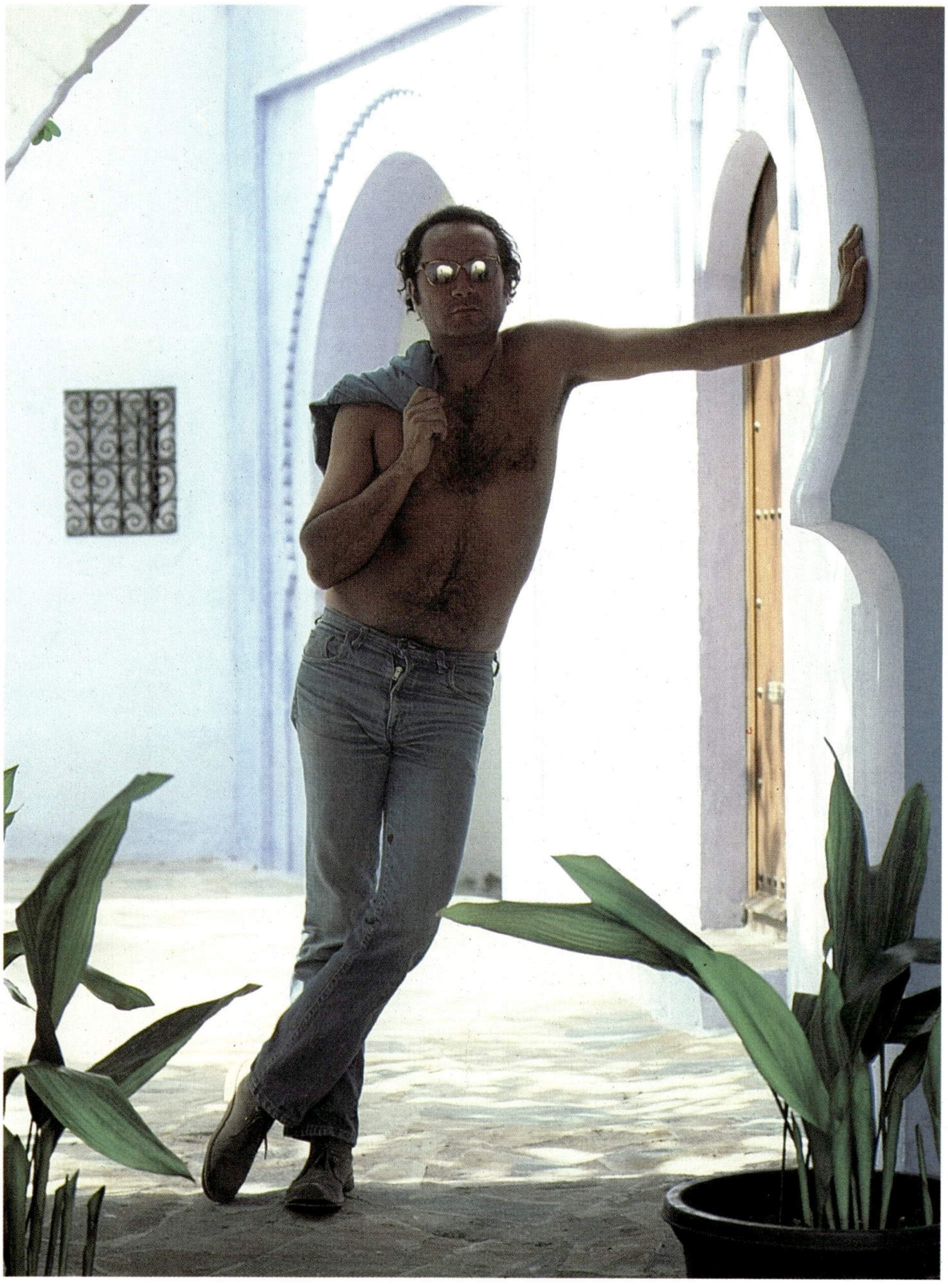

The man has a sweet and gentle air
Casual in his faded jeans
What is he doing in the village?
Nothing is as it seems
His glasses give him a mysterious look
Of one that thinks and dreams
What goes on inside his mind
And could I be part of his schemes?

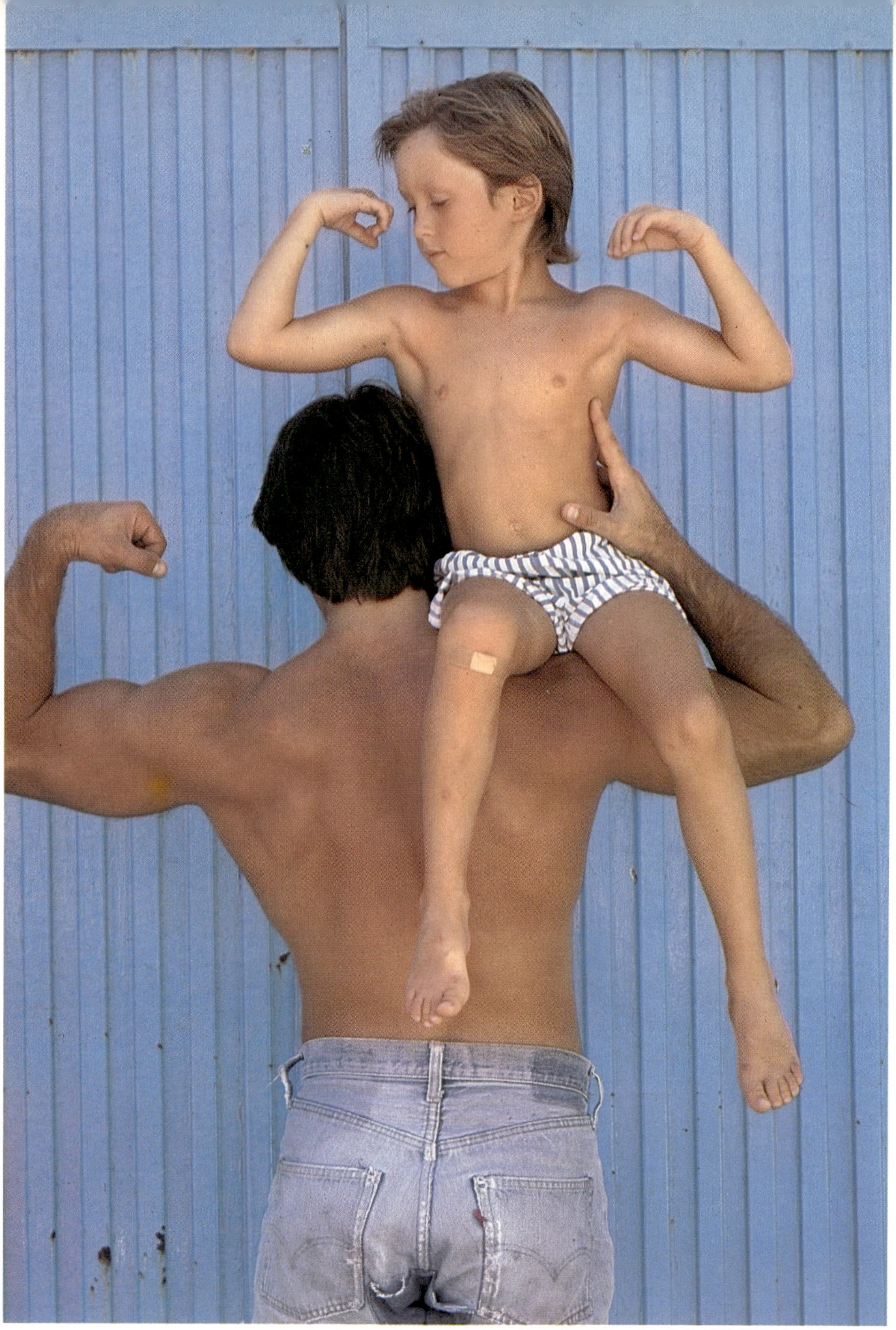

Thank heaven for little men
Even if they're only ten
They grow up in the most delightful way
Or so they say
... But I'll take the big one for today

This young man is quite a lad
Although he's really not that bad
I've known young men of many types
... But underwear with Stars and Stripes?

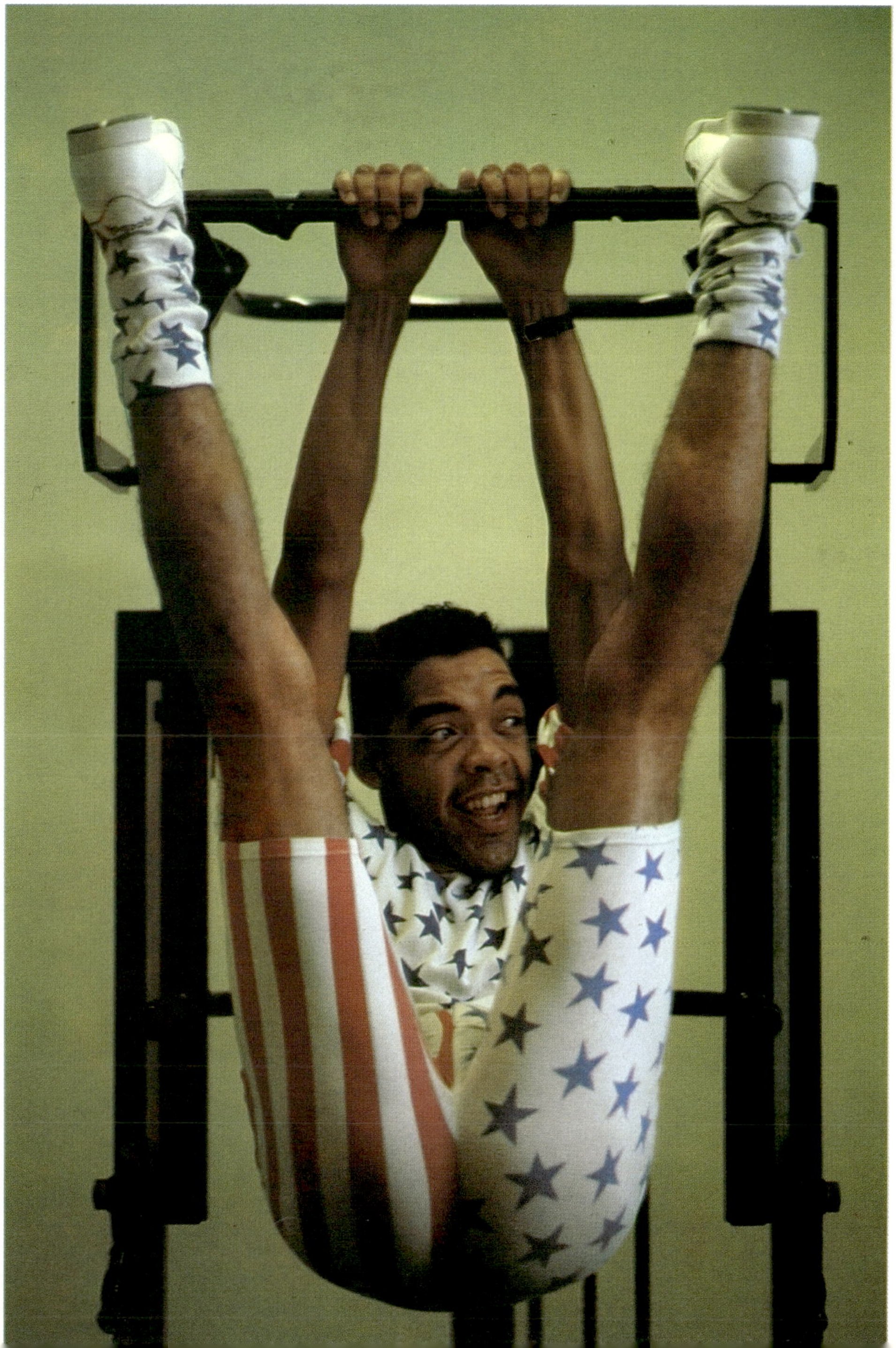

I saw this young man from afar
As I drove past him in my car
The wild wind blew right through his hair
He didn't seem to have a care
He looked the type who just runs free
... I wonder if he'd run after me?

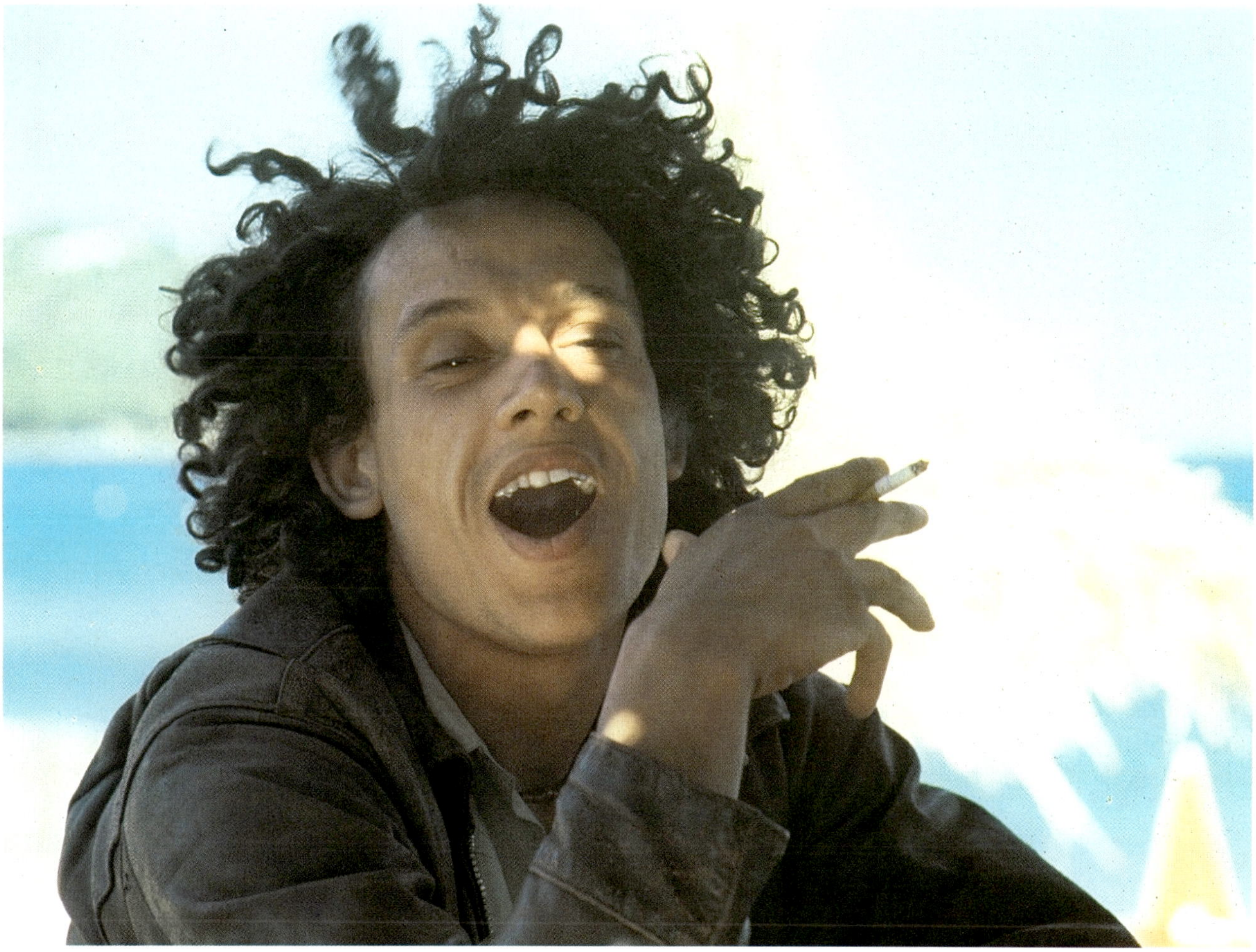

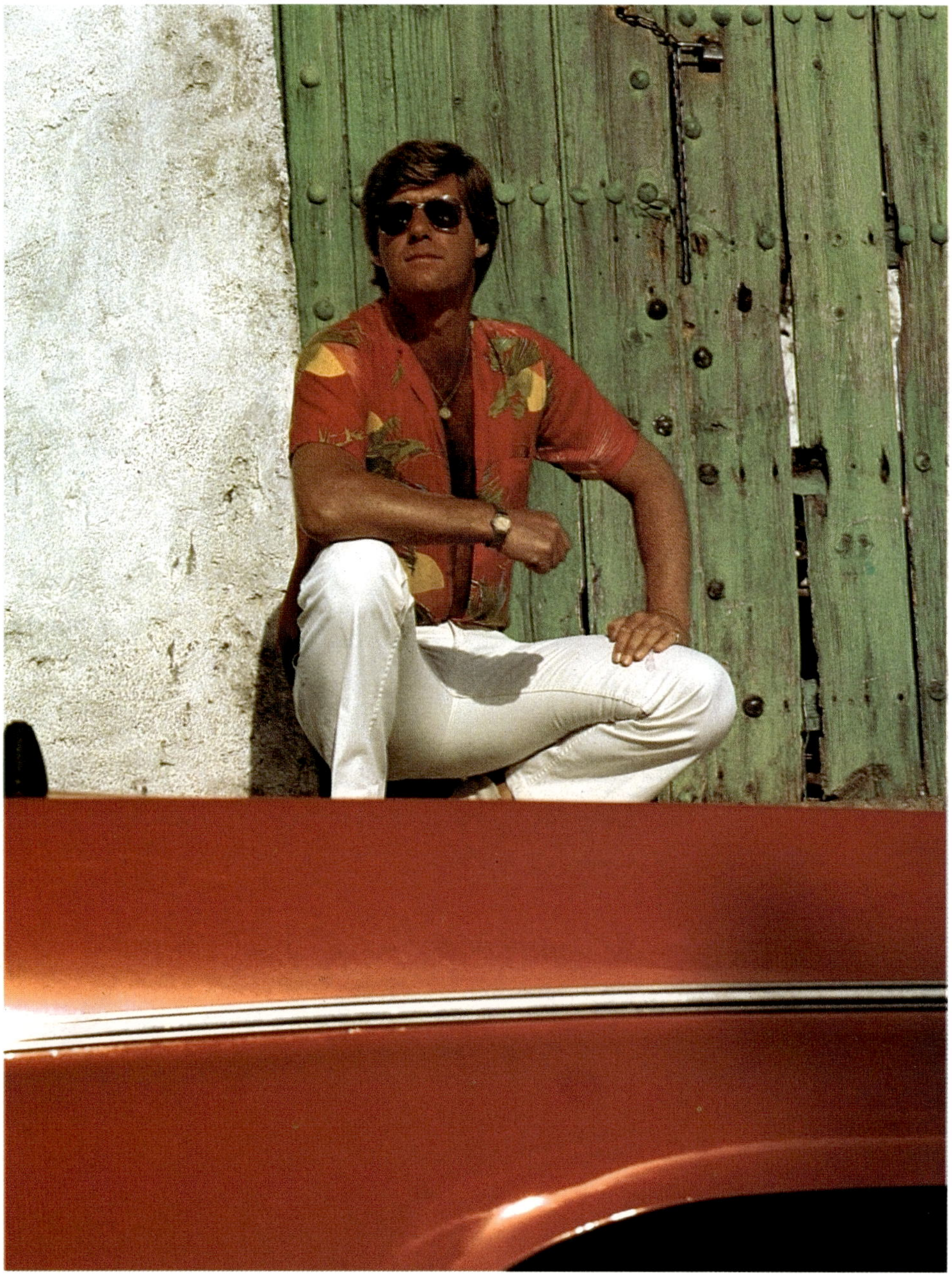

Red shining car and sparkling chrome
This colourful man invited me home
I didn't have a thing to lose
But I wished he'd take off those strange white shoes

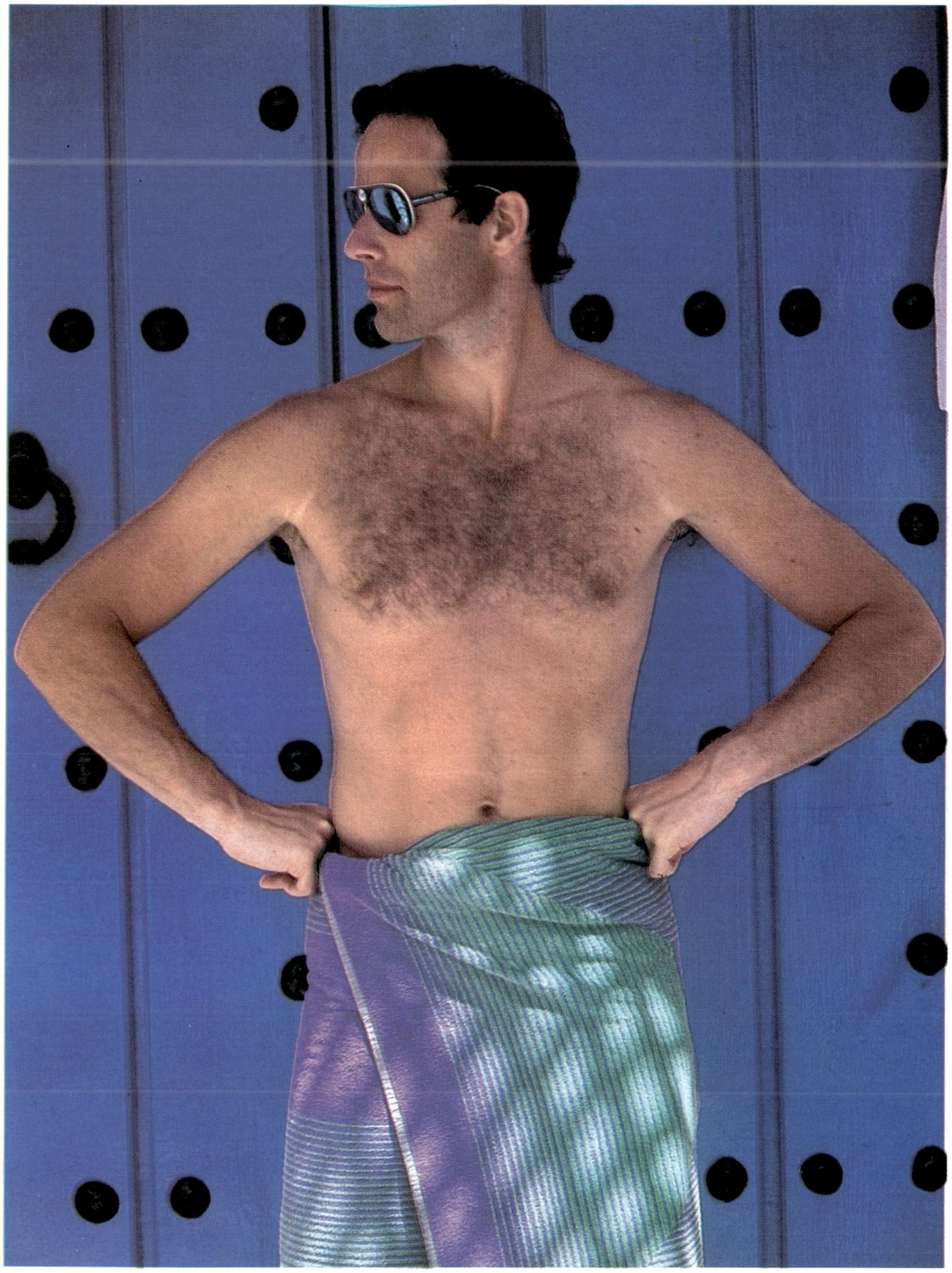

The young man was on the prowl
Clothed in nothing but a towel
What would happen if it fell down?
... We'd know if he were man or clown

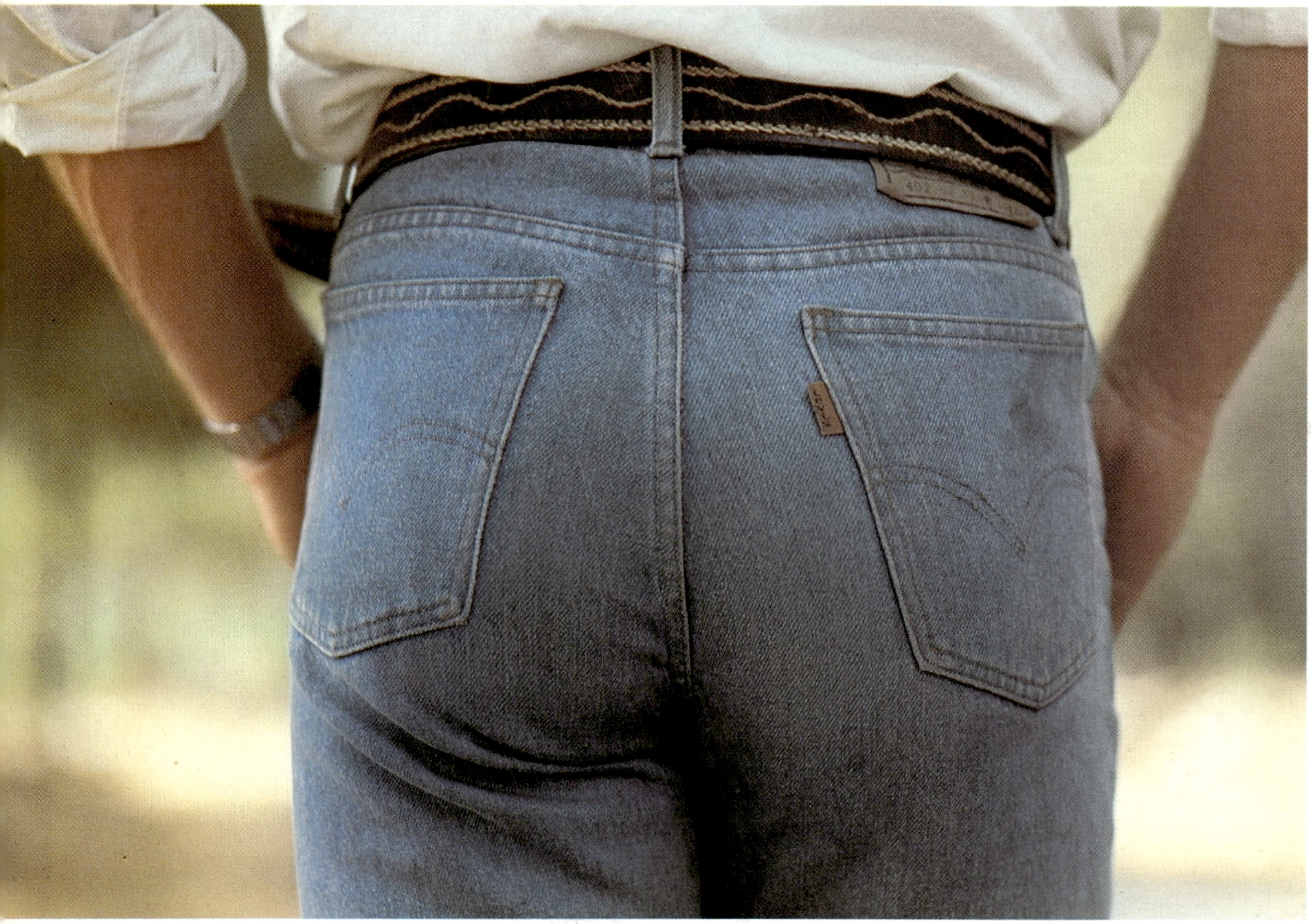

Standing there
he had an air
of savoir-faire
debonair
a certain flair

But I must declare
I could only stare
at his blue-jeaned derrière